Respectful Parenting:

From Birth Through the Terrific Twos

Joanne Baum, Ph.D.

Child & Family Press • Washington, DC

Child & Family Press is an imprint of the Child Welfare League of America. The Child Welfare League of America is the nation's oldest and largest membership-based child welfare organization. We are committed to engaging people everywhere in promoting the well-being of children, youth, and their families, and protecting every child from harm.

CHILD WELFARE LEAGUE OF AMERICA, INC.
HEADQUARTERS
440 First Street, NW, Third Floor, Washington, DC 20001-2085
E-mail: books@cwla.org

CURRENT PRINTING (last digit)
10 9 8 7 6 5 4 3 2 1

Cover design by Jennifer Geanakos
Text design by Pen & Palette Unlimited

Printed in the United States of America

ISBN # 0-87868-764-5

Library of Congress Cataloging-in-Publication Data

Baum, Joanne.
    Respectful parenting : from birth through the terrific twos / by Joanne Baum.
        p. cm.
    ISBN 0-87868-764-5
    1. Parenting. 2. Parent and child. 3. Child rearing.   I. Title.
HQ755.8 .B3686 2001
649'.122--dc21

2001047019

Dedication

To M.J.M.

Contents

Acknowledgments

I want to thank someone I never met but who greatly influenced my thinking about parenting—Harper Lee, the author of *To Kill a Mockingbird*. I read that book more times than I can count when I was growing up. I loved what Atticus Finch told his daughter Scout: "To really know a person, you've got to get in their shoes and walk around in them for a couple of days." Little did I know that Atticus was sowing the early seeds for Respectful Parenting.

In high school and early college, I worked in the Special Services Department of the Samuel Field YM/YWHA, in Little Neck, New York. The director, George Singfield, became an early role model, mentor, and lifelong friend, whose work I have always greatly admired.

In graduate school I was privileged to work with Dr. Carl Whitaker. We did co-therapy with families in his seminar for psychiatric residents and in his practice at the University of Wisconsin. Carl always encouraged me to trust my instincts, be creative, meet the family where they were, and shake up their apple cart so the apples didn't come back down in the same place. He believed all people could grow and change.

Another old friend and professional colleague, Dr. Carole Campana, read a much earlier version of another manuscript I was preparing. I had started writing anecdotes of my first couple of years as a mom, thinking parents would like something humorous and real they could relate to during those five-minute potty breaks you sometimes get from your young child. Carole read the first 50 pages of material and called me, excited. "This is great stuff. You have something here. You're treating Matthew differently than anything I've read about. What's your theory?"

"Theory?" I asked, confused.

"Your theory behind what you're doing with your child. It's different than what I've ever seen before. I've read hundreds of developmental psychology books and you're onto something here. If you could include some ideas as to *why* you're doing *what* you're doing, this would be a fabulous book." Carole spurred my thinking, and my theory became *Respectful Parenting.*

The theory of Respectful Parenting actually developed slowly over the years, not only with my own child, but with people who came into my office and shared their lives, their struggles, and their growth with me. Through my work with them, I saw the need to modify old ways of parenting so children could grow more confidently into adults who believed they were worthwhile—the need for a new underlying philosophy of parenting. Respectful Parenting grew out of the clinical work that took place in my office. Sometimes it was difficult, sometimes it was magical, but always it was intriguing and challenging. I want to thank everyone who came into my office.

I want to give heartfelt thanks to the parents who allowed me to interview them so I could include more examples of respectful parenting. This book is much richer because of their stories and anecdotes.

To take the time off from my practice so I could write, I needed support, which was generously provided by Leo and Arvila Berger. It was my dream come true—I could write full time. Thank you Leo and Arvila for the gift of time to think creatively and produce this book.

On the more personal side, I would never have started this project in its initial form, nor had a mother's perspective on Respectful Parenting, without my child and all he has added to my life. Being Matthew Jacob McCarthy's mom has been a joyous, creative, and sometimes challenging experience. I wouldn't have had my child if not for my husband, Tim McCarthy. Tim has been very supportive of Respectful Parenting, in theory and in practice. Thank you both for coming into my life. You are both dearly loved.

My parents, Bill and Elaine Baum, and my sister, Karen Baum, provided me with a strong family of origin to begin my lifelong quest of learning, loving, and appreciating those significant people around me. My parents have grown up beautifully, even as they helped me grow up. I wouldn't be me without them.

And last but not least, there's the Child Welfare League of America. Sue Brite left a thrilling message one day on my answering machine, saying she was interested in publishing the book and hoping someone else hadn't gotten to it first. Sue was the first one to recognize its potential. It has been a pleasure to work with Peggy Tierney as an editor. She has believed in this book, provided a fresh perspective, and had a vision of what it would look like. I truly appreciated her insights. I'm very glad the staff at CWLA saw this as a worthy project.

Introduction

Respectful Parenting was developed during years of working with individuals, couples, and families in my private practice. Many of those people had been raised in alcoholic homes. If not alcoholic, their home had usually been "dysfunctional" to one degree or another. The people who walked into my office had acquired their "emotional baggage" in various ways, but the end results were very similar. They had low self-esteem, and they didn't have a clear picture of what they deserved in life. They felt unhappy and dissatisfied. They came for therapy because they had an inkling that life could be easier, less painful, perhaps even happier—but they didn't know how to get there.

Sometimes I could simply talk about options for their lives and they could put them into action. Others could see options, but something stopped them from acting on possibilities. It was like their past emotional scars were preventing them from moving forward. Sometimes I used "reparenting" techniques with adults in order to heal their painful childhood memories. By giving them options of what their parents could have said and done, and playing out old scenes with these new options, they were able to see, feel, and hear what it would have been like if they had been parented respectfully.

When they experienced what it felt like to be parented respectfully, they were able to balance their memories, give themselves new options, and feel less pain. They were also able to understand their reactions from childhood and forgive themselves for their own behaviors that had gotten them in trouble. They could view those old behaviors as strong survival patterns and feel proud of themselves for coming up with new ways of coping. They were able to stop sabotaging themselves.

The next step was for them to learn how to treat themselves with respect. They learned to listen to their own needs and to take themselves seriously. They learned to consider options and their merits before jumping into something. They learned to curb their self-criticism and to assess themselves with greater gentleness. They gained self-appreciation.

After they were feeling better about themselves and looking at life differently, then we'd deal with how they were parenting their own children. They had to slow themselves down from an adult time frame to their children's. When they slowed down and listened very carefully, they were able to avoid reacting on automatic pilot and instead asked themselves, "How do I want to react today, as an adult with all I've learned in my life?"

As I worked with these adults, they healed themselves, parented their children differently, and healed themselves further by feeling good about how they were parenting. They were able to raise children with healthier self-esteem and prevent their family tradition of pain from continuing. The key ingredient was mutual respect rather than forced compliance through fear and intimidation.

After years of going through this process with people, a light bulb went off. If we could parent respectfully from the beginning instead of waiting to help adults who were feeling bad about themselves, we could avoid a great deal of pain and we could raise healthy, happy children into healthy, happy adults. That's how the theories and ideas behind Respectful Parenting were born—I was instinctively developing and teaching these ideas before I knew intellectually and conceptually what I was doing.

Respectful Parenting

We are going to assume that if you're reading this book you're one of the millions of people who said as they were growing up, "Just wait till I have kids. Boy, am I going to do it differently!" or "I'll never do that to my kid." Unfortunately, as many of you may have found out already, parenting differently than you were parented is not as easy as you once thought. Let's examine why.

Role modeling is the most powerful way we learn. Role modeling means that what you see and observe is what you learn. In other words, all your life you've picked up on the behavior you see around you. You have remembered and in essence learned from the scenes that occurred around you from the first day of your life. All that you have seen and experienced is embedded in your brain. These experiences, available to you in your conscious and unconscious memories, will come out in your actions whenever you react to something automatically.

If you had a healthy, positive childhood experience, then that is a very good thing. You'll pass along those good parenting techniques that you learned from your parents. However, even the most enlightened parents of a few generations ago had very different expectations of children and very different ideas of parenting than what we have today.

At the turn of the 20th century, American culture reflected Victorian era philosophies about child rearing, which were summed up in the expressions "Spare the rod, spoil the child" and "Children should be seen and not heard." The first expression not only condoned but recommended hitting children to prevent them from becoming "spoiled." In a sense, the Victorian era was about breaking children's spirit so they would be "seen and not heard."

In the early 20th century, children were to be responsive to their parents' needs. They were expected to have a certain demeanor that did not allow for boisterous behavior or making demands for themselves. It is clear that surviving took most of the parents' efforts and time. People's life expectancies were shorter and their work was often physically taxing. Parents weren't concerned with maximizing the quality of their lives or their children's lives. Back then, you were being a *good parent* if you kept a roof over your children's heads and food in their bellies. There wasn't a lot of time or energy for *frivolous* things like nurturing. Besides—that might lead to your child being *spoiled.*

In addition, up until 100 or 150 years ago, children—and women— were looked at as possessions of their parents (or husband), without any legal rights of their own. Women and children were allowed to be beaten by men as they saw fit, and children could be exploited in any number of ways. What has changed in the underlying philosophy in the last century is the view of children as people in their own right and not merely extensions of their parents, and deserving of their own limited legal rights, legal protections, and personal freedoms as well. Laws were created, such as those preventing child abuse and those providing for the prosecution of parents for murdering or abusing their children—even laws in the case of children who are successful in the entertainment business, dictating that the children's earnings be kept in trust instead of being spent by their parents. As society's view of children as possessions changed, we experienced an evolution of parenting along the same lines—instead of existing for their parents' needs or pleasures, children are seen as individuals with needs and rights of their own.

Those Victorian days were really only three or four generations ago. In some families that would have been your great-grandparents and how they treated your grandparents. Your grandparents—who had been raised with rigid disciplinary guidelines to prevent such horrors as *spoiled children*—would have raised your parents, who, in turn, raised you. Thus, the "Children should be seen and not heard" and "Spare the rod, spoil the child" philosophy is not so far removed from your life. I'm going to call this type of parenting "old-style parenting."

Today, however, there is wide recognition that early messages, both positive and negative, affect people throughout their lives. The first few years of a child's life do leave indelible messages in a child's psyche.

The first popular and widely acclaimed child development specialist to influence people raised by Victorian-era parents and grandparents was Dr. Spock. His early books became popular in the 1950s. Although his ideas later changed, in his early work he encouraged rather rigid schedules for eating and sleeping, along with watered-down versions of Victorian-era disciplinary practices. Many people raised like this went on to raise their children along the same lines, but others rebelled against the rigid routines and went in the opposite direction, giving into their children's demands and whims. Some people talked until they were blue in the face and then acquiesced. During the 1960s and 1970s many people were influenced by the "hippie" movement and adopted a *laissez-faire* parenting attitude. In more extreme cases, this attitude became benign or not-so-benign neglect, often influenced by parents' drug and alcohol usage when they attempted to cope with familial responsibilities by "getting high." These parents forgot that children need boundaries and limits along with negotiations at appropriate times.

Respectful Parenting is a balanced, child-centered approach, which is healthy not only for the children, but for the entire family. On the one hand, parents will recognize that not only adults, but children have feelings and needs of their own, including the need to feel respect and some degree of control over their lives. On the other hand, the respectful parent realizes that children need boundaries and discipline in order to feel safe and secure, to receive guidance on the choices they make in their lives, and to adapt successfully to the world and its demands on them as they continue to grow and develop.

When you're respectfully parenting your child, you're viewing your child as a young human being who deserves your respect, appreciation, consideration, time, and love. You see your child as someone you can learn from, someone you can learn with, and someone you can teach things about life. Your parenting decisions and actions are predicated on a basic belief that you and your child will give each other respect and understanding. You will set limits, but they'll be reasonable, negotiated when possible, and you'll give a warning before you act on them. Respectful Parenting is time consuming and takes a lot of energy. But it's worth it, because parenting in this way rewards both you and your child on many levels.

Old-Style Parenting vs. Respectful Parenting

Here are a number of old-style parenting lines many people report to have heard when they were growing up. These often resulted in hurt, shame, fear, or guilt on the part of the child and later the adult he or she became. Do any of these sound familiar?

"If you don't stop crying, I'll give you something to cry about!"

"I'm going to kill you if you don't stop...."

"Because I said so, and if you don't do it now, you're in big trouble!"

"Why are you doing this to me?"

"How could you be so stupid?"

"What's wrong with you?"

"You're a bad boy/girl!"

"How come you can't be good like David/Debbie down the street?"

"Do you ever think before you do anything?"

Think about times you've heard a parent "demanding" that their child listen and respect them. Even by demanding this, the parent is being "disrespectful" to the child. Why should the child respect a disrespectful parent? And how is the child going to learn how to respect another person if he or she is not being treated respectfully? A person must see a behavior and be exposed to it a number of times to be able to do it on one's own. Respectful parents realize that we must be role models for how we treat others and how we want others, including our children, to treat us.

Here is an example: let's say a parent has said, "Johnny, go wash your hands, it's dinnertime."

"I don't want to," Johnny replies.

The parent immediately responds, using an angry tone of voice. "I told you to go wash your hands! Now listen to me!"

"But they're not dirty," the child implores.

With more anger, the parent responds, "Stop talking back to me. How dare you be so disrespectful. I told you to go wash your hands. Now go do what I said right now or you won't get any dinner."

"But why?" the child replies reasonably. "They're clean."

And the parent might very angrily reply, "Because I told you to. Now that's it! You go do what I told you to right now or absolutely no dinner!"

Where along the way was that child's reality taken into account? The parent repeatedly demanded adherence to the rules, but did not stop long enough to consider the child's point of view. In situations like that, the child will often comply out of fear, but fear and compliance are very different from respect. In this example, the child could easily go off to the bathroom, sullenly muttering (disrespectfully) under his breath...and why not? By being disrespectful to the child, that parent was perpetuating the negative behaviors he or she was trying to stop.

Instead, the following respectful conversation could have resulted in hands being washed and the child being taught some basic respectful behaviors and hygiene at the same time:

"Johnny, would you please go wash your hands? Dinner's almost ready." (A less harsh request with a respectful please.)

"I don't want to."

"Why not?" (listening to child's opinion and validating it by addressing it instead of just ignoring it).

"I'm playing."

The parent walks to where the child is playing (again, respecting child's reality). "Oh, I can see that. Well, dinner is just about ready. How about washing your hands and eating, and then you can come back to play some more after dinner?"

"But they're not dirty."

"Let's see . . . why you're right. I don't see any dirt on them either. But you know what? Unless you've just washed them, it's still a good idea to wash your hands before eating, even when you can't see dirt, because sometimes teeny, tiny pieces of dirt or germs can be there even though you can't see them, and they might get inside your mouth and body when you eat. So, for health reasons, it's a good idea to always wash before you eat."

"Oh, okay," the child says somewhat reluctantly but understandingly.

"Thanks for listening," the parent might say cheerfully, reinforcing the child's cooperation. Or, if the child had recently washed up, you might simply say, "You're right, they do look clean. Thanks for showing me. Come on in and eat." Again, you'd be validating the child's reality, and at the same time, you'd be modeling how to be respectful. On the other hand, you don't want to have this long conversation about hand washing every time you ask your child to wash his hands. If you've gone through this before, you would use a shortened version: "Remember we've talked about germs and hidden dirt and washing your hands before eating?" Hopefully, your child would nod or say something about remembering, and you could add, "Well, here's your opportunity. Go ahead and then we'll eat."

Another example: A 2-year-old decides he wants to get out of the other side of the car from where his parent was sitting and is now standing, holding the door open. He normally gets out the closest door, but now he's standing by the far door and clearly wants to get out that door for a change.

Old Style Parenting: The parent stands at the customary door and says gruffly, "No, I'm not going to walk around the car. You come here." The parent's tone of voice sounds unnecessarily harsh, as if this little 2-year-old had said something inconsiderate or disrespectful. The father's tone of voice implies that the 2-year-old's behavior (wanting to come out the other door) is somehow wrong or bad.

Respectful Parenting: "Oh, okay. Do you want to see what it's like to get out on that side of the car?" Or, "Sweetie, see all my packages? It would be easier for me if you'd come out this way right now. We'll try it your way next time when my arms are free."

It's true that the shortest distance would be for him to come out your way, but who says we have to be totally efficient at all times? With old style parenting, the child was reacted to in anger and the message from the parent's gruff tone of voice was, "How dare you request such a thing!" or "What's wrong with you?" or "Who do you think you are? I'm not going to walk all the way around the car for a (mere) 2-year-old." The child was not "being bad" with his simple request, and he didn't need a negative interpretation put on his simple request.

By accepting your child's request, the respectful parenting response lets him make a choice of his own and role models being respectful of someone else's wishes. He saw what getting out the other side of the car was like, and within a short period of time, he'd probably be back to getting out the side you opened. Your son can be listened to and respected. It's no problem, just a few steps. If your arms are loaded and you've been respectfully parenting all along, he'll go along with your idea because you've gone along with ideas of his in the past. Again, you've role modeled how you want to be treated. Children of respectful parents will sense your interest, your love, your caring, your awe, and your respect. When they feel it from you, they'll be able to give it back to you when you want to be listened to as well.

If You Had a Traumatic Childhood

Respectful parenting offers you a way to improve on how you were parented and to heal some of your old hurts along the way. That is not to say that we should throw the baby out with the bath water. With very few exceptions, it wasn't all bad, but you can make some improvements—especially in areas you remember thinking, "When I'm a Mom (or a Dad) I won't. . . ."

Unfortunately, as many of you may have found out already, parenting differently than how you were parented is not as easy as you once thought. Let's examine why. As stated earlier, role modeling is the way we learn, especially how to parent. Your parents were, by their behavior, role modeling how to be a parent to you. Thus, you are living with the reality that what you saw when you were growing up has been programmed consciously and unconsciously into your brain. The things your parents said and the things your parents did will come out of your mouth and hands automatically, the good with the not-so-good, like tapes being replayed.

That's why you may find yourself saying things and doing things you swore you'd never do. In extreme examples, it's why we see adults who were physically abused as children growing up to abuse their own. It's important to realize that those old, familiar tapes are very strong. Any changes you want to make are going to have to be concrete, conscious choices on your part. While people from healthy, loving homes can often rely on their "intuition" to parent in a healthy, loving manner, you may not be able to do that. Remember, your brain has stored all your life experiences, and it can only supply you with the options it has on hand, no matter where your heart is. If you were not parented respectfully, your brain cannot give you that option unless you have seen it someplace else or you learn how to do so now.

Luckily, the strategies and techniques of respectful parenting can be learned. The strategies provide the framework you'll need to come up with new, healthier parenting options. You'll probably have to practice them a few times before they begin to feel natural. You'll be learning how to stop the old tapes and replace them with healthier alternatives so you can fulfill your promise of being a different parent to your children than the parenting you experienced growing up.

You'll certainly be healing old wounds left over from your own childhood, healing your "inner child" by hearing and watching yourself treat your child in ways you wish you had been treated. An "inner child" can be thought of as the keeper of your childhood memories—the images, feelings, sights, and sounds you experienced as a child are stored inside of you. It is the place where your early vulnerable and insecure feelings are housed. The young person you were back then, when the hurt first happened, is still there, still needing what it didn't get and waiting for someone to come along who can provide what it's been waiting so long to receive—love, respect, compassion, and understanding. When you respectfully parent your child, you will be validating your own feelings—by parenting as parenting ought to have been done for you. Your self-esteem will improve by recognizing how well you are parenting. You'll get respect from your child by giving him or her your respect. You'll get lots of hugs and appreciation in return for giving lots of hugs and appreciation.

You will also rekindle old positive memories that you had forgotten as you hear yourself saying or doing things that, on some primitive level, feel familiar. Sometimes old, bad memories overshadow the good ones, but the process of growing up and growing beyond your childhood will be aided by remembering the things that your parents did right. It's a wonderful feeling, after doing something sweet with your child, when you intuitively know that what you just did with your child was done for you. Your inner child will feel nurtured by your actions with your own child.

Your inner child, the place where your early joys and excitement with life's discoveries are housed, is ready for you to tap into the energy you felt when you were little, to once again enjoy the old joys. It's waiting to be validated when you rediscover some of the happier moments from your childhood by doing something with your child today that taps into something positive from your past.

Respectful Parenting Strategies

A philosophy can intellectually explain what's happening, but it doesn't provide you with tools to change. The strategies suggested by respectful parenting give parents direction and guidance. They provide the framework you'll need to come up with new, healthy parenting options. Some will seem very broad, others will seem specific, but there are plenty of different techniques you can do within each of these strategies.

- **Begin with a stance of learning with your child and learning from your child.** In other words, be a mutual learner rather than a know-it-all teacher. You'll eliminate the one-upmanship and inherent power struggle of old-style parenting.

- **Slow down.** This cannot be stressed enough. An adult's pace of operating in this world is very different from the pace of an infant, a baby, a toddler, or a small child. You will miss too many cues from your child when you are going too fast. We know you're trying to fit a lot into your day, but it will actually go more smoothly and you'll accomplish more when you slow down. If you find yourself saying "what" or "hurry up" repeatedly, slow down.

- **Listen carefully, using all your senses.** See, feel, and hear what your child is saying. This is important not only for your preverbal child, but even for school-aged children. In spite of verbal abilities, children often have difficulty articulating their emotions. This is why psychologists often have children draw what they are feeling. You'll get a more accurate and complete message when you use all your senses to listen.

- **Listen with the idea that you're willing to change or compromise your ideas if your child suggests something you hadn't considered.** If your child offers a good alternative to your plan, be flexible and do it his or her way. You don't want to do this every time, because then your child will think he or she is running the show and that isn't healthy either. But children like the idea that they have some control over their lives and will be much more cooperative. By following your child's lead instead of imposing your own agenda every time, you'll be led into that slow-moving, enchanting world that children can help you rediscover.

- **Focus on your child.** So often, we interact with our children while thinking of something else. If you are preoccupied, you will misinterpret or miss signals from your child. Focusing on your child will help you to understand completely what he or she is feeling and make your child worthwhile and important.

- **Be in awe *with* them.** Recapture the innocent delight in life that babies and small children naturally have at their disposal unless it's been scolded out of them.

- **Be in awe *of* them.** Appreciate their perspective of the world. See how terrific they are. Feel how excited they are. Hear how involved they are. Feel how incredible it is that your little one is learning all about the world.

- **Give your child positive messages.** Rather than saying "Don't spill your milk," say "I like how carefully you're holding your cup." Our brains often ignore negative words like "not" and end up doing the very things we want to avoid. Wording messages positively helps assure you of the responses you want.

- **Validate your child's ideas.** You can do this by listening carefully, commenting on her input, eliciting her input, and doing what she wants when you can. You can tell what a preverbal child wants by watching her facial expressions and listening to the types of sounds she is making.

- **If you don't like how you're viewing your child's behavior, refocus your view.** By refocusing your view you're looking for another, more positive angle to view the current situation. When your child cries in the middle of the night, feel good that your child trusts you enough to cry out for what he may need rather than being angry that your sleep is interrupted.

- **Look for the positive intent in your child's actions.** If your child pulls all the plastic containers out of the cabinet, look at it like a game he's trying to play with you rather than extra work he's trying to create. Laugh with him and then show him how much fun it can be trying to get the containers back in the cabinet. See if he can hand you one and then commend him for his help. Have fun with him.

- **When you're in a power struggle with your child, back off for at least 30 seconds.** By backing off, you'll clear your mind a little and remind yourself that you're the adult here and you need to give the situation another look rather than being caught in a power struggle with an 18-month-old. There's always a different way to handle the situation rather than head on. Backing off gives you the breathing room to figure out a more creative solution to the dilemma at hand.

- **Don't sweat the small stuff.** Think about whether creating an uncomfortable situation is worth pursuing. Save your creative energies for the big stuff. If your toddler will not leave the buttons on your phone alone, just move the phone. In a few months, those buttons won't be so tempting and it won't be an issue anymore.

- **When you're feeling stuck about what to say or do or when you're about to say something you don't want to, quickly give yourself a time-out.** When you take a time-out, even if it's only a minute to breathe deeply, you'll be clearing out the old automatic response and allowing yourself to think clearly about how you want to respond.

- **When in doubt, ask for help.** Sometimes we can't see the positive options ourselves, and sometimes we are just human and need a break. Hopefully, there'll be someone around either physically or by phone whom you trust. If you're religious, you can pray. If not, it can still be very helpful to just say out loud into the air, "Help, please!"

If You Had a Traumatic Childhood

If you are a parent who is healing from a traumatic childhood, here are some additional strategies and some reinforced strategies stated previously.

- **Give yourself messages using positive wording.** Instead of saying, "I don't want to hit my child" or "She's driving me crazy," tell yourself, "I'm going to take the time to slow down and accept the fact that my baby is having a bad day. I can tell her that I wish I knew how to help her, but that until I do, I can at least hold and comfort her."

- **When in doubt, ask for help.** This is especially important for you. When you ask for help, you're in essence surrendering from the struggle you're in where you don't see a way out. When you give up the struggle, all kinds of new options may come flooding in. And, parenting can be a lonely business. It always helps to have someone to share with and hear how someone else dealt with the same problems.

- **Acknowledge when you do things well.** Keeping a journal can provide you with ongoing feedback on your life as a parent. It can reinforce those techniques that work with your child, and it reinforces positive behaviors on your part. If you don't like writing things down, at least give yourself some verbal positive feedback rather than taking your efforts for granted.

- **Celebrate your victories.** When you handle a potentially difficult situation well, get an image of what life would have been like for you as a child in the same situation and congratulate yourself for handling it better.

- **Forgive yourself when you "slip."** When you forgive yourself for not being the perfect parent, you will free up a great deal of energy that can be used to be a much better parent from today forward.

- **Enjoy the process.** Many positive changes are going on in your life—changing your behavior as a parent, watching your child's reaction, feeling better about yourself, and healing your inner child. Savor these changes. Why is this parenting thing so difficult? You have your own personal history you're bucking, combined with your parents' personal history, combined with their parents' personal history, and so forth. That's a lot of momentum. To understand your parents and forgive them for their mistakes, it is helpful to look at how they were parented. To look at how they were parented, it's helpful to look at the prevailing parenting philosophy at the time. When you forgive your predecessors for what they have done and how that has affected you, you can forgive yourself for not being the perfect parent and free yourself to gather a respectful, creative, and useful bag of parenting tools.

But let's remember it's not all about forgiving and understanding your parents and your own mistakes and foibles. As you examine where they came from and how they parented you, hopefully you can find some things to celebrate, both in how far they came, in what they learned, and how they treated you. If you're reading this book and looking at how to be a healthy parent, then somehow a desire to grow, to entertain new ideas, to try things out, was instilled in you. Your parents gave you some other good things, too. Remember those and celebrate them as you go. By appreciating their good qualities, you'll also be role modeling how to accept people for who they are. Even though we're focusing on what you want to improve or change from how you were parented, please keep in mind that whatever you went through, it wasn't all bad, although there's always room for improvement. We can go for progress but not perfection. Please keep that in mind when you're critiquing your past, and hopefully your children will keep that in mind when they critique theirs.

Nursing

O ne of the first decisions a soon-to-be family makes is whether the mother will breastfeed a new baby. In the past, this wasn't a decision that parents carefully deliberated, but rather was a given: mothers nursed, period. It was often a matter of survival. Nursing became more of a choice when formulas for bottle feeding were developed. Advertising declared that it would be easier and more reliable to prepare a "scientifically developed" formula in bottles rather than to nurse a child. Bottle feeding became the vogue, while "old-fashioned nursing" went by the wayside.

Breastfeeding began to make a comeback in the 1960s and for good reason. The benefits of breastfeeding are irreplaceable. An infant needs immunoglobulins from a mother's breast milk, because his own supply is not adequate for at least six months.[1] That is partly why Dr. William Sears writes, "Breastfeeding is the ideal feeding relationship for you, your baby, and your family."[2] Nursing also protects the baby from such things as diarrhea, respiratory tract infections, ear complications, and allergies. Orthodontists believe that breastfeeding contributes to the proper alignment of your infant's jawbone.[3] Breastfeeding protects babies by strengthening their immune systems so they are better able to fight germs. Breastfeeding offers your baby a strong sense of security by providing a smooth transition from prenatal to postnatal life. Breast milk changes as your baby changes to continually supply the most nutritionally sound source of nutrition. It's easy to digest. Nursing your child is really the most nutritionally sound way of feeding your baby and it's the most nurturing beginning you can provide your baby. Yet, we are seeing a continued decline in the number of women who breastfeed their newborns and who nurse for more than six months.

If You Can't

From a nutritional and nurturing standpoint, nursing is definitely the best thing you can do for your baby. This chapter will discuss the advantages of nursing and give some parental anecdotes about the nursing process. But it is important to acknowledge up front that for various reasons, not everyone can nurse their newborn babies.

Today's working women are also finding it difficult to breastfeed as long as they would like. They don't have private places where they can relax and pump milk during the work day to keep their milk supply up. Some can't take the time to pump at work. Some women find it difficult (or impossible) to relax enough within a 30-minute or even a one-hour lunch break, to eat and pump. Many are forced to cut back on their nursing and only nurse in the morning and night. Others say the stress of trying to juggle all of life's demands cuts down their milk, they become frustrated, and so do their babies.

In these circumstances, women often feel guilty about not being able to live out their breastfeeding dreams. They really don't need that guilt when they're doing the best they can to juggle work, home life, and a personal life. So, if your breastfeeding "career" is not exactly what you had hoped for, first seek advice from experienced mothers or through such resources as La Leche League or lactation consultants listed in your yellow pages before giving up. If your individual circumstances can't be modified, please accept the fact that you're doing the best you can, given life's reality and let go of the guilt. You and your husband can always give your baby plenty of cuddles and loving, even if your baby isn't nursing.

Jeanne: I tried to breastfeed for two weeks on and off, but it was clear she preferred the bottle. I had to admit she had made her choice and I had to stop trying to convince her that my preconceived notion was the way to go. I realized I had my agenda, she had hers, and she was perfectly happy without breastfeeding. I was causing her frustration by trying to get her to like something she had no interest in.

When I finally made the decision to stop trying to nurse, I could see a big difference in me: I relaxed more, accepted her decision, and now, six months later, I feel terrific. I don't think it did anything to our "bonding." If anything, because I respected her choice maybe I was telling her something. She's a cuddly baby, so she certainly gets her share of hugs, holding, cuddling, and touching in all those important ways.

For you parents who can't or choose not to breastfeed, please don't feel like you're cheating your child or giving her an inadequate beginning. If you provide your infant and small child with lots of cuddles, loving, hugs, understanding, and respect, your child will have a wonderful, healthy beginning. If you are looking at adopting a baby and think you can't breastfeed, please check with La Leche League in your area. They may be able to help.

If You Can

For women who have a more flexible work situation, nursing for as long as your baby wants is feasible, enjoyable, and beneficial for both you and your child. These women say nursing helps them maintain a balance in their life. They're able to quickly make the switch from "working woman" or "professional woman" to Mom, by sitting down and rocking and nursing their child soon after they come home in the evening. They view nursing as a relaxing, nurturing time for both themselves and their child. These women often believe in a child-led weaning process, rather than parent-led weaning.

Penelope Leach, in her book *Your Baby and Child* (1989) says, "Many first-time mothers find the first few days worrying, strange, and uncomfortable; as a result, some abandon the attempt to breastfeed within a week of the birth. Don't give up before you have given yourself a chance to experience the glorious times ahead when these early problems (of breastfeeding) are over and the milk is there, like magic, whenever the baby wants it."[4]

Sarah: I'll never forget those first few seconds of actual contact. It still amazes me how an infant knows instinctively to latch on and nurse without anyone having to teach him. Seconds from being fully nourished through an umbilical chord, never having used his mouth or throat for taking in food, there he is, peacefully sucking away. A truly miraculous endeavor, if you ask me. And that a woman's body can provide such incredible nutrition and nurturing all at once is equally miraculous.

Unfortunately, women often feel pressured by well-meaning friends and relatives, particularly those who were parenting in the days when doctors unanimously recommended formula feeding, and breastfeeding was looked at as primitive and degrading. Stick to your beliefs and your child's needs; feel comfortable knowing that all the scientific evidence is behind you. Contact other breastfeeding mothers or organizations if you start to have doubts.

Sarah: Despite my attitude and my husband's support, it was still rather difficult when my mother-in-law came for the first time. Our baby was 3 weeks old, and the doctor said that his intestinal tract was still undeveloped and causing him to cry. Within hours of my mother-in-law's arrival, she had deduced that I must not have enough milk and proceeded to tell me that she had tried to nurse her oldest child, but hadn't had enough milk, and I was going to have to face that fact, too. I listened to her, but tried not to say anything. Finally, at the end of the day, after hearing this numerous times, I said, "Look I don't think it's a problem of not enough milk. He's gaining weight beautifully. I'm not worried." I think my tone of voice, which was not the sweetest, put her off a little, and that was all we said on the subject that day.

The next morning, when our baby started crying again shortly after he had nursed, she said, "You're probably right. It's probably not that you don't have enough milk. It's probably that you have too much milk. You should supplement your feedings with formula; then you wouldn't produce as much, and he wouldn't be uncomfortable.

I just stared at her thinking, "I thought you were coming down to help. I don't need this. I don't need anyone chipping away at my self-confidence as a new, nursing mother." The third time she brought her new theory up, I said, "I don't think I have too much milk. I don't think there is such a thing as too much or too little milk. I've seen a lactation consultant and I've talked to the La Leche League. Please, I'm not going to supplement my nursing with formula. I'm committed to this for at least six months. There are good reasons why I'm doing this. And the doctor thinks his intestines just need some more time to develop. And that's all."

She did feel strongly enough to respond, "Well, what do you expect? The La Leche League! Don't they advocate nursing? That's their mission! What do you expect they'd tell you?" I just had to let it be, as I didn't have the strength to argue any more.

Of course, what she didn't see was my crying later, when I was overtired and scared that maybe my beliefs weren't accurate; but after talking to the La Leche leader again, I stopped doubting myself. By 3 months, all our baby's gas was gone, his intestines were fully developed, and we were still happily nursing away with my milk being his only nutritional intake.

Strategies for Successful Nursing

- **Slow down.** This cannot be stressed enough. An adult's pace of operating in this world is different from that of an infant, a baby, a toddler, or a small child. You will miss many cues from your child if you go too fast. Your day will actually go more smoothly and you'll accomplish more when you slow down.

- **Drink lots of water, eat really well, and take vitamins.** Nursing and producing nutritious milk are very demanding on your body, so you should take good care of yourself, both for you and your baby.

- **Follow your child's lead whenever possible, rather than imposing your own agenda.** If you nurse when your baby wants to rather than imposing your own schedule, life will run smoother for you and your baby. Your baby feels hungry when his little tummy is empty, and he will stop nursing when his tummy is full. Sometimes your baby will want to nurse for comfort, and what a wonderful way to comfort and nurture your child. Your baby will end up being calmer, happier, and less fussy if you follow his needs for nursing. Sometimes babies have a "nursing strike" for a few days and don't seem interested. Simply offer every few hours, and if your baby isn't interested, don't worry. Usually babies want to return to nursing within a day or two, having tried a bottle and finding it lacking. They may miss the closer nursing and come back to it. If not, then your baby has led you into, through, and out of your nursing relationship, and it's just fine to calmly follow his lead. When you follow your child's lead, you're telling him on an unconscious level that he has good ideas. You're helping shape his positive self-esteem by letting him know he's worthwhile.

- **When in doubt, ask for help.** Hopefully someone whom you trust will be available either physically or accessible by phone. You can also call trained lactation consultants listed in the phone book or through La Leche League.

Your Schedule

An added benefit of nursing is that it can actually make your life easier in some ways. When you're going out for a few hours, you don't have to worry about taking bottles and formula—you have your milk in place. Likewise, if you find yourself and your baby stuck somewhere unexpectedly, feeding your baby is not a problem. When your baby voices her "I'm hungry" cry, you just find someplace to sit and quietly provide what she needs. An added benefit is that nursing produces a relaxing hormone for you, so as you nurse and relax your baby, you also calm down.

For example, when my infant was 4 weeks old, I joined a group for mothers and their infants offered by the local adult education program. After the second group, I suggested to a few mothers that we go out to lunch at a restaurant across the street. They thought it was a novel idea and with some trepidation we set out the following week. There were six of us and six infants, the oldest being 8 weeks. All was fine until one of the babies started crying. The mother looked upset and asked, "What should I do?" "Nurse her," I said. "Here?" she asked, blanching as she looked around. You have to understand. The restaurant was full, packed with the lunch crowd, and besides our table, there was not a customer under at least 60 years of age because the restaurant was in a small shopping center at the entrance to a large retirement community.

I said, "What choice do you have? Otherwise, you'll have to leave and you just ordered." It made sense to me. She said, not too enthusiastically, "I guess I could try..." and she lifted her blouse, as discreetly as possible. Her baby latched on happily, quieting down immediately.

Within 15 minutes, and from then on, at least four of us were nursing at one time. Far from disapproving, I don't think any of those older folks left without stopping by our table to comment on how wonderful or delightful it was to see young people in there, or to see young mothers nursing again. They all hoped we would be back. What a pleasant surprise for us. I know it helped me by "launching" my public nursing in such an accepting and approving atmosphere.

Fathers and Breastfeeding

Cindy: People don't talk about it often, maybe because breastfeeding families are supposed to be so excited about the wonderfully close, nurturing beginning they are providing their child, that they aren't supposed to be anything but ideally happy about their situation...but breastfeeding can cause tension in a marriage. I know it has in mine. Don't get me wrong. My husband and I are both committed to it, and we know in our heads and hearts this is the right thing to be doing. But periodically my husband says things like, "You know, I know it's great what you're doing with our baby, and how much time you're willing to let her nurse. But I miss you! You're in there with her, sweetly nursing her to sleep every night for 45 minutes or so, while I'm out here twiddling my thumbs and waiting...Sometimes you fall asleep, too, and you don't come out here to the living room to join me at all.

We used to have our evenings together and now we get so little time, just the two of us. And no, I don't want to lie beside you two and watch her drift off to sleep. That's okay now and again, but every night it's boring and frankly, whether it's cool or not, I'd rather watch TV. But you've got to know that sometimes I'm jealous and I don't like that you're so dedicated and I'm supposed to be so damned dedicated, too. And sometimes I feel left out. I know how terrific it is supposed to be to watch and know your wife is doing this wonderful thing for your child. And most of the time I feel that way, but sometimes...I just don't. And those times I wish you'd stop nursing already."

I can see his point. I really can. Sometimes I'm sympathetic to him, and try to accommodate him, or at least sympathize. But other times, I react angrily because I'm scared he's going to start really pressuring me to stop. I want to nurse till she wants to stop, not till my husband wants me to stop. I'd really resent it if he pulled a power play like that and insisted . . . I don't really think he would . . . but even his not-so-subtle suggestions tear me up inside. I love nursing her. I know he needs me, too. But he's an adult, he needs to wait. And so sometimes, it's difficult.

I think the term "estranged" would describe it. We are growing apart in some ways, so I think there is a little-talked-about downside of nursing that ought to be acknowledged and talked about more. I can't believe we're the only couple experiencing these kinds of mixed feelings and strains.

Fathers sometimes do feel left out when a mother nurses her baby, especially if the nursing relationship looks like it's going to extend beyond infancy or those first critical six months that are supposed to ward off later allergies and strengthen your baby's immune system. But if you can view your family as a nursing *family* rather than a nursing mother and child, the father doesn't have to feel so left out. If he understands the benefits of nursing and can see how healthy his baby is, then he can often be more supportive of the process. It is also helpful if the mother can pump extra milk so Dad can feed the baby sometimes and feel that special closeness involved with feeding the baby. Most people say to wait to pump until your baby is 6 to 8 weeks old so you establish a strong nursing relationship before introducing the bottle, because the baby can get milk faster with a bottle's nipple and may get confused or prefer the nipple if it's introduced too early. So, Dad has to be patient for a while.

In his book, *Becoming a Father*, Sears writes, "Breastfeeding is a lifestyle, not just a method of feeding. Providing understanding and support for the breastfeeding pair is one of the most valuable investments you can make in the future health and well-being of your family."[5]

Conclusion

During the 1950s and early 1960s, the possibility of beginning your life with a close, warm physical relationship with your mother, as she quietly breastfed you, was not an option at all. Technology and the medical community's stance opposed and prevented it. Only with the rise of the feminist movement, the environmental/ecology movement, breastfeeding support groups, and women who were thinking for themselves and more willing to do what happens naturally, has nursing enjoyed a resurgence.

How much more nurturing can you be than holding your crying infant in your arms, bringing him or her close to your warm body, providing the kind of comfort that only closeness and intimacy can bring, and at the same time, providing the benefits of perfect nutrition? Okay, so some people will question why you're nursing and not using bottles. Others will question why you're "still" nursing. Others may even be embarrassed. But if you, your baby, and your partner are in agreement and sharing the benefits of a nursing "family," you'll come up with some creative responses when the situation arises. Remember to look to your baby for cues. When you see him resting peacefully in your arms, nursing himself into a blissful sleep with a perfectly calm face, free from anxiety, you'll know there's no need to stop.

To Spoil or Not to Spoil

This cannot be stressed enough: There is no such thing as "spoiling" an infant. Children may be spoiled when they are given everything they want, but **an infant does not have any wants, only needs.** A clean diaper, food for an empty tummy, even being held are all needs of an infant. An infant communicates his or her needs by crying, and an adult can be assured that she is taking care of all the baby's needs by responding to a baby whenever he or she cries.

As we have already seen, people used to fear "spoiling" a child. They truly believed you could ruin a child at an early age by responding too much when an infant cried. Today, child development specialists caution against worrying about such things in early parenting days. Instead, we advocate that parents stay tuned in to their children's needs and provide uninterrupted nurturing geared toward the specific developmental stage of the baby's life.

It is sad that so many children were raised with a regimented feeding schedule instead of being fed when they were hungry. Think about it. A baby's stomach is small and needs frequent feedings, but babies raised with rigid schedules were forced to wait through painful crying spells and empty tummies until it was convenient for their parents.

You are not just caring for the physical needs of a baby when you respond to her cries; you are taking care of emotional development needs as well. When you convey a deep, strong, continual love toward your child, your child will feel good about herself and will be more likely to behave in a desirable way. Let's look at adult needs for intimacy, for comfort, for closeness, for human contact. Most adults, when they marry (if not before), sleep together. Why? Because they don't have enough beds to sleep apart? No. Because they like the comfort, the softness, the intimacy of cuddling or being close to another human being they care about. Did they develop that need at the altar, or when hormones raced in adolescence? No. Most human beings are born with a need for closeness.

One woman who came to me for therapy had become a mother in the early 1970s. She experienced a great deal of family pressure to maintain rigid feeding schedules and give fairly limited comfort to her crying baby. She was repeatedly told to "just let him cry it out." But she felt something was wrong. Intuitively, she wanted to respond to her son's cries more lovingly. Sadly, because of her own personal background of physical and verbal abuse, she was unable to follow her instincts in the face of her husband's threats, her in-laws' advice, and her parents' disapproval. She was ridiculed for being a baby herself and not realizing that this infant "had to learn" to wait until his next mealtime or to comfort himself.

She reported the following:

> I could hear my son crying and wanted to go to him. He was so small, so defenseless. Yet, when I'd start, my husband would berate me for spoiling him. I often got as far as his closed door, where I would sit on the floor and cry quietly, wanting to have the courage to go in, but afraid of defying my husband, my in-laws, and my parents, who demanded that I teach our son that he was the child and we were the parents, and we would say when it was time to eat and when it was time to play. I hated it, but I did it.
>
> Now I know I taught him not to listen to his own instincts and that he wasn't important. By the time our son was 17, our whole family was in therapy so we could unlearn those early oppressive messages. I was relieved that finally someone was telling me that my more loving instincts had been right. Maybe we'll have a chance of becoming a

healthy family. I just hope it's not too late for our kids. I don't want them to repeat what my husband and I passed down to them from our parents.

Dr. Marianne Neifert, in *Dr. Mom,* warned people not to make the mistake of thinking that a "good" baby is undemanding or that a demanding baby is "bad." She offers the perspective that a demanding baby is a healthy baby, presenting you with opportunities to teach your baby that he's loved and can count on you. If this information had been available when my client was a young mother, she might not have had to suppress her loving instincts and adopt her family's more rigid, stern approach. The rigid parenting techniques and ensuing pain that reigned in her family for the next 17 years could have been avoided.

In close, respectful parenting relationships, babies seem to take a lot. Outsiders who don't understand what's going on wonder about parents who "give, give, give." By giving, the parent is establishing healthy building blocks for the baby's self-esteem. Parents who are parenting in this newer way feel so rewarded by their child's appreciative responses that it's easy for them to keep giving. The simplest guideline I can offer parents is: respond lovingly to your child's needs when he or she expresses them.

Some of today's parents see that as a ridiculous request. They're still afraid of "spoiling" their children. Often well-meaning parents and in-laws try to influence and/or pressure you with their perspectives. It's difficult to buck those pressures, but if you and your baby's other parent are in agreement, you can. Others may say things like, "You have to impose a feeding schedule on an infant as soon as possible." Newer parents need to remember that it used to be the goal to have a child fit into your world and to meet your needs, the needs of the adult. But that isn't the goal anymore.

> **Linda:** Never before in my life did so many people have so many things to tell me about how to run my life. It mostly had to do with my baby. I shouldn't hold him as much. I shouldn't nurse him as often. I shouldn't coddle him. I'll spoil him. I'll tell you, if it hadn't been for those nightly teary discussions with my husband who felt the same way I did, I

don't think I could have gotten through those first few weeks of well-meaning friends and relatives. The ones who agreed with me were reassuring, but the others really tested my confidence as a new mother. I had my instincts, which said to hold my baby as much as I wanted and to respond to him immediately, but I also knew my background hadn't been so good and I didn't want to go overboard in the opposite direction. It really helped a lot that my husband knew about this stuff from his work and continually reassured me that I was doing a great job, even better than he had imagined. I don't know where I'd have been without his support. Now that my baby is 10 months old, everyone says I have such a happy baby—even some of the same people who tried to get me not to hold him just a few months ago. It's funny, but now I just tell myself, "They mean well," and I do what I believe is right.

In *Dr. Mom*, Marianne Neifert suggests what a healthy parent should do in order to prevent intimacy problems in adulthood.

When [an infant] has a need and it is satisfied, he learns that the world is a safe place and he is loved. By trusting, he begins to learn to communicate...Follow your instincts and hold, hug, talk, and attend to your baby without limits. You CAN'T overdo it. If you are excessively affectionate, you'll end up with a responsive, secure, happy baby who knows he is loved and will love in return.[1]

Crying—or Communicating?

When a human infant cries, he's telling you something. A child doesn't cry without a reason. Crying can be an intelligent form of communication. As stated before, we recognize today that infants have no wants, only needs. These needs are felt and expressed in an urgent fashion. And, more importantly, the needs should be taken care of in a timely, loving way. Needs only go away when they have been taken care of—they cannot be ignored away.

It's important to learn what your baby's cries are saying. If you're not sure, pick him up so you can see more clearly what he's trying to tell you.

If he stops crying when you pick him up, there's your answer. If not, then go through the basics: is he telling you he's hungry, needs to be changed, tired, or simply wants some closeness and comfort? Those are the four biggies. If your baby is still fussy, simply talk to him calmly about what is surrounding him in the world. Talk him through his fussiness.

If You Had a Traumatic Childhood

I have worked with people whose needs for closeness have been suppressed by childhood traumas. Their only defense was to erect rigid, impenetrable boundaries around themselves. Or others who were left alone so much as infants and small children, they suppressed their needs for closeness to mask their pain from such early rejection and abandonment. These circumstances notwithstanding, most adults do need, desire, and enjoy some degree of closeness with other adults even though they have knowledge, experience, and tools to cope with life's stresses. Why wouldn't a newborn infant, a baby, a toddler, or even a small child who doesn't have these resources to "make himself feel comforted" be entitled to the same, if not a lot more?

Yet it can be very difficult for people who were raised the old-fashioned way—left to "cry it out" or responded to with anger or frustration—to come to understand that babies' cries are an expression of needs rather than an unreasonable demand for attention. How can an adult relate to this? Have you ever really needed to go to the bathroom? It is a physiological need. It can't be put off. It must be responded to immediately. That's what an infant has—immediate needs that must be responded to quickly. And when a parent respects those needs by responding lovingly and understandingly, the infant begins to learn two vital things: her needs *can* be met and she is capable of *getting* her needs met. You may be doing the "work" for a while, but the infant learns she has the personal ability to get her needs met.

Many adults never developed those two basic beliefs themselves. These adults usually share some of the following beliefs: they don't believe they can get their needs met, they don't think their needs are legitimate, they think they're not capable of getting their needs met, or, worse still, they don't believe they deserve to get their needs met.

Life often has supplied these people with family members, friends, lovers, partners, or spouses who have told them their needs are not important, that they're being demanding or ridiculous. Is it a coincidence that certain people find these kinds of unresponsive mates? I don't think so. When parents ignored their child's crying as an infant and small child, when they made that child wait until it was convenient for the parent to take care of him or her, and when those children learned to subliminate their needs to their parents' schedule, the children learned they were not worthwhile or important. If you add the gruff parental one-liners from Chapter 1 to these nonverbal messages, the end result is wounded adults who do not see themselves as worthy or worthwhile. Those early messages set them up to find people in their adult life who will repeat those kinds of invalidating messages so life feels normal and familiar on an unconscious level, even though consciously they may feel hurt, alone, and inadequate.

Learning to parent differently will produce two positive results. First, your baby will be calmer, less fussy, and less demanding the more secure he feels, and she will eventually be a much "easier" toddler. Second, you will enjoy a greater closeness with your child than you shared with your parents, a rich love that grows out of emotional give-and-take.

The Long Term

When you take care of your child's needs, your child may seem overly dependent in her early development. She will probably stay close to such a loving mom and dad because she knows she is safe there and that her needs will be met by these people. As these children grow, they have confidence in themselves. They're more confident in venturing out into the world around them. Over time they learn about the difference between needs and wants. They're able to satisfy their needs and understand that their wants sometimes go unanswered. They seem to have more patience, perhaps because they have a deep-rooted trust in others and can wait for things to happen without a panic reaction that, once again, just like way back when, nobody will be there. They have a level of self-assurance, what we call high self-esteem, that allows them to venture off and feel good about themselves.

All this because they were nursed or fed on demand? All because they were held when they needed to be? It may not be the only reason—but what a wonderful foundation! What a terrific way to begin to learn so many things: I am loved, I am terrific, people respond to me, I am appreciated, they think I'm important, they love me, they can do for me, I can do for myself, and I can do for others.

While you were growing up, a child who thought or said these things would have been accused of being "egotistical" or having a "swelled head." How absurd that a child who legitimately thinks he is unique and special would be criticized. What's wrong with appreciating yourself and feeling good about yourself? It's not the people who feel good about themselves that do all the boasting as teens and adults. People who truly feel good about themselves often tend to be more humble about it. They know who they are and are often generous with others. No, it's those who feel poorly about themselves who try to cover up that reality by boastful talk and actions. The boasters are not people who have an underlying healthy self-esteem, nor have they been loved, held, coddled, appreciated, or respected as infants, babies, toddlers, and young children.

A child who is respected and loved, who is responded to on demand for the first year or more, will be a calmer, happier toddler and grow up to be more self-assured and happier than a child who is forced into your schedule and whose needs obviously take the back seat to yours, the parents. There is plenty of time later on, after establishing this healthy internal base, for the child to learn the differences between needs and wants, to learn about waiting. Children will learn these lessons. They'll also realize that other people in this world deserve compassion, understanding, and respect. They will know how to do that from what Mommy and Daddy taught them through role modeling. And they'll probably take the time and effort to find friends who will treat them well, because they know they deserve to be treated that way.

> **Sarah:** When my son was not quite 3 years old, I had to leave him to go to my grandmother's funeral. I explained to him that I would be leaving him with his daddy for a few days because Grandma had died. He asked me why she had died, and I told him she had been very old and frail and just didn't have the strength to live anymore. I reminded him of how

small she had been when we last saw her, and told him a little about how she used to be and why I had loved her so much. He knew she hadn't been able to hold him six months before when we had visited because she was so little and frail. So he had some understanding. He even assured me that he and Daddy would be okay.

About a week after I came back, he and I were in the bathtub and he said to me, "Mommy, when you're old and little, I'll hold you and take care of you." My eyes filled with tears as I gathered him in my arms and hugged him. "Really, Mommy, you hold me and take care of me when I'm small, and when you get old and small, I'll take care of you." What a sweetheart he is. I hugged him and told him that would be lovely. I was in awe of his understanding and ability to know that, someday, I, too, would be old and need help.

Learning with Your Infant

This chapter covers the earliest time period in your child's life, from birth to this first developmental milestone when your infant becomes a baby. The word "new" is the key here. Your infant is new to this world and you are a new parent to this baby. Even if this is your third or fourth child, you don't know this unique infant, and you need to take the time to get to know each other. Introductions were made in the hospital—now come the "getting to know you" phase.

Strategies

- **Slow down.**

- **Listen carefully, using all of your senses. See, feel, and hear what your child is telling you with different cries and looks.**

- **Be in awe *of* them and in awe *with* them.**
  Recapture that innocent delight that babies naturally have at their disposal. Appreciate their perspective of

the world. See how terrific they are. Feel how incredible it is that your little infant is learning her way around the world. Be in awe that your baby knows to seek out new information and to naturally go for what's safe (you). When your baby feels your awe, she feels pretty important, wonderful, and appreciated—and her self-esteem blossoms.

- **Follow your child's lead.** Respond quickly and lovingly to your child's needs.

Everyone Is Learning

The first couple of months with your infant are characterized by intense learning on everyone's part. Usually your learning takes place through bleary, sleep-deprived eyes as your baby's personality begins to emerge. You're learning how your infant communicates his needs so you can physically and emotionally take care of him. Plus, you're trying to take care of yourself and keep up with your family's needs. An exciting juggling game is going on as you maneuver your way through what may be the biggest transition of your life. While you're going through your changes, your infant is contending with his own changes. After nine months of slow, steady growth in a warm, darkened place, where nutrition was available automatically at all times and sounds were muffled and muted, your infant has been thrust into an entirely alien territory.

It's pretty amazing when you look at an infant's need to learn and adapt to survive. From the moment your infant is born and the umbilical cord cut, everything is new—not a single thing resembles what was before for your infant. So, if you're feeling like everything is new and a bit overwhelming, imagine your infant's feelings and remember: she doesn't have the tools, resources, or world experience that you have. From this perspective, it's certainly much more understandable why an infant cries to be held—a sense of connection from being held is vital for establishing a sense of security.

A parent can unknowingly create a negative cycle. An infant cries. The parent picks up the infant to comfort him. The parent's arms are rigid because she's not sure why her infant is crying, or whether she'll be able to comfort her. The infant feels tension and tightening in the parent's body as she's being held. This doesn't feel soft and safe. The infant reacts by crying more. The parent hears the infant crying while trying to help and feels even more insecure and inadequate. The parent may clutch the infant more frantically, worrying about what's happening and not being able to fill the infant's needs. The infant feels the parent's increased tension and intuitively knows something's wrong and cries more. The sad part is, each person is trying to communicate with the other, but it's not working.

Bonnie: I was so tired one night, I didn't think I could go on, yet there she was crying again. I nursed her, but she still cried. I rocked her and she still cried. At that point I felt myself tensing up. I had an urge to shake her. Wow, that's how child abuse must start. I could see how it was possible at that moment. I was so frustrated and tired and clearly at the end of my rope . . . but I didn't shake the baby. I could have, but I didn't. Instead, I called out to my husband, who was in the study.

I needed help. I was too tired to calm down, or be the kind of parent I wanted to be. By the time he came in, both the baby and I were crying.

I told him I needed a break and asked him to please take over. I needed to sleep. He tried to calm me down, but the baby was wailing by now. I told him I'd be fine. He didn't need to worry. I just needed some sleep. And I needed him to take the baby and calm her down.

He looked a little anxious. I was able to say, "You can do it. I know you can. I need to sleep."

It was the first time I was faced with my physical limits affecting the way I wanted to parent. I knew it wouldn't be my last. I was glad I had learned quickly to ask for help instead of trying to force myself beyond where I could lovingly go. And I'm grateful I was able to get some much needed help.

Later, when I did wake up, I felt refreshed. My husband and baby were playing together. I was able to gather my happy infant in my arms, give her a few kisses, and apologize for being so tired and probably feeling cranky to her earlier. Her eyes just sparkled away in response. My parents never said they were sorry or acknowledged the effects their behavior may have had on us kids. I want to do that with my child.

Communicating With Your Infant

New parents can relax and convert their anxious energy into loving, concentrated efforts: look at and listen to your infant, rather than being in your head, with fear and insecurity blocking your attempts to figure things out. Listen to your intuition. You have studied your baby like no one else has. Early parenting is easier when you follow your infant's cues.

When what you're doing is *not* working, my other suggestion is to try to slowly talk your feelings through with your baby. Not just short statements like: "I'm getting frustrated because you won't stop crying," but the process behind your feelings. If you slow yourself down, your tone of voice will be calm instead of anxious. For example, "I love it when I can hold you and you stop crying, but here we are. I'm holding you, and you're still crying. It's not your diaper, I've checked that. I just tried to feed you, and you don't seem to be hungry because you turned your head away. I wonder what it could be. I wish I knew. Imagine when you can talk, and you'll be able to tell me. Here you are, so little, trying to let me know something. This can be so frustrating. There, there, I'm listening. I want to help. I just don't know how. Hey, your cries are getting lower. You feeling better? Did you just need some extra time and talking? Maybe you just wanted some human contact. Oh, look at that big yawn. That's so sweet. Big stretch. That was it. You woke up and couldn't quite fall back to sleep. Thanks for letting me know. I'm glad to have been able to help you. Now, you're peaceful again. Ahhhhh."

This kind of talking is soothing to you and your infant. It allows you to slow yourself down to your infant's pace and communicate your concerns. As you talk, your baby may be soothed by your caring tone of voice and stop crying. You may be reassured by calmly going through what you're trying and the effects. New options often flood in when you slow yourself down and process. Your arms may relax as the negative, tense cycle reverses itself. Infants do not understand words, but they do respond to tone of voice and physical feelings, like a gentle body lovingly holding them.

In addition, by sharing your process with your infant, your words and actions are congruent, and that's important to your infant's developing sense of trust. An infant is incredibly sensitive to subtleties in non-verbal and verbal communication. For instance, if you are saying, "There, there, everything is fine," but your arms are holding your child with a tense rigidity, your infant knows on an intuitive level that something is wrong and she can't relax. In graduate school, counseling professors say, "There are no rules about communication except you can never *not* communicate." Assuming that's true, you may as well communicate positive, loving, appreciative messages from the start. For instance, you can thank your infant for all she is bringing into your life. By the time a baby understands words, she will have "gotten" that she is adequate and worthwhile, that she brings joy to other people, that she does things other people appreciate, and that she has a positive influence on the world around her. Those are the lessons she'll learn from what you've communicated with her. You'll also be introducing her to manners (when to say thank you) from modeling yourself.

Some of you may be saying, "What you're saying right now sounds okay, but not for an infant. I'll wait till my child is old enough to understand—say 4 or 5—before I'll talk like that." If you wait that long, you'll probably never start because other parenting techniques will be in place. You'll have practiced avoidance for so long, it will be difficult to switch. Worse yet, the damage will be done. You'll have been sending mixed messages that have confused your infant, baby, toddler, and small child for so many years that your child will have learned that grown-ups don't mean what they say. Your child may have trouble developing a solid sense of trust and security.

Slowing Down and Taking Cues

Raising infants and small children involves surrendering many adult ways of looking at things. The more childlike and spontaneous you become, the more you'll enjoy your infant. Likewise, the more you slow down, the more you'll notice and appreciate. If you don't focus on the minor actions and changes your infant is making on an almost daily basis, you'll be missing a lot of growth, excitement, and transitions. These small but momentous happenings make all the diapers and all the late-night feedings worthwhile.

> **Sarah:** I'm still in awe of all I learned and continue to learn by watching and being responsive to him. It's been his lead; he's taught me. I remember saying to my husband, "How can this 24-hour-old infant teach me so much? I read the books and he just is." So far it's been the nicest, most loving education I've ever received. I just never knew I'd learn so much from him so quickly.

I can remember the simple joy and loving exhilaration of playing with my child when he was 2 months old. I remember fun times, sitting with my back against the bed frame or couch arm, my knees up. Supporting his back as he sat perched against my thighs. My arms helping to balance him if he shifted his weight enough to warrant that. We talked and "played" for as long as three-quarters of an hour at a time. Those goos and gurgles and coos were some of the best conversations I'd ever had.

Sometimes we'd throw in tongue thrusts, arm waving, and singing, just to vary our repertoire. There I was, the "professional woman" turned into the "rhapsodically happy mom," thrilled at these small but significant early communications with my child. In those first few days, weeks, and months, he taught me about simple, joyous fascination. I hope I never forget his early teachings.

You may be so bleary-eyed from lack of sleep that focusing on anything can be difficult. Try starting with little things such as smiles, coos, hand movements, eyes following objects, and hands reaching for objects. Your enthusiasm will be giving your infant valuable feedback, telling your infant he is worth paying attention to, a good learner who is learning to manipulate his environment, fun to be around, and downright

Games You Can Play

- Hands touching hands

- Sitting up with your knees providing a back for your child. Have your hands in place to help balance your baby. Look into her face and make a sound she likes.

- Handing her a small, easy-to-hold object

- "Fetching" something she drops

- Mutual tongue movements

- Bubble kisses

- Sharing simple toys, first in black and white, then with primary colors

- Sitting and looking out a window together with your baby on your lap. Point to things and explain. A window can be a slower moving form of visual stimulation and easier to cope with than the television.

enjoyable. These early lessons contribute to your infant's self-esteem. It's never too early for that kind of feedback.

Bonnie: I learned to slow down. I've always been a planner, but with my daughter I couldn't plan my day, because when I did, I ended up being frustrated and it just wasn't worth it. For months, it seemed like every time I thought we had a routine, she'd change it. A few times, I almost wished I could impose more of a feeding or sleeping schedule on her. But then I'd look at her cherubic face and know I'd rather alter my lifestyle then have her crying until her needs were met.

I learned I had more choices than I ever imagined. If I didn't get the laundry done one day, there was always tomorrow. If the house was messy, oh well. If dinner wasn't cooked, we'd get take-out food. The one thing I could guarantee was, when I was able to shed my expectations, I'd have a great (although possibly exhausting) day with my daughter. Without plans, I left myself time to adore her and revel in her infant antics when she was awake. When she was asleep, I could look at her peaceful face before falling asleep myself or take the time to get something accomplished around the house.

Parenting High-Need Infants

A number of years ago I was doing some observations in a day care center. I noticed a little 5-month-old girl who was crying throughout the day, despite being held and talked to quite often. One day, I asked an experienced infant care provider if it was ever difficult to keep providing her with hugs and soothing talk because they often didn't seem to have much impact. She wisely responded, "Oh no, not at all. I know this baby is trying to tell us something. It seems like, for some reason, her little world doesn't feel too good to her. We may figure it out one day. Or who knows, maybe she'll always be the squeaky wheel and get herself heard. But, for whatever reason, she needs a lot more loving and understanding than the quieter infants. If we keep giving her cuddles and understanding hugs, she'll sense our love and acceptance, and it'll all catch up with her one day."

It took a long while. This child didn't smile freely or easily for about a year and a half. She didn't cry all that time either. From about 7 to 18 months, she took her surroundings in carefully, participated with other children at times, but often sat back and watched. Sometime after that, I noticed a tiny little girl looking up at me with a radiant smile. I almost didn't recognize her. It was the little girl who used to cry so much. The loving had caught up with her. The last time I was observing at the day care center, she was 3 years old, still smiling, and had formed playful relationships with several of the other children. She was not a "squeaky wheel." The caregiver had been right. All that extra loving and acceptance (rather than frustration and anger) caught up with her.

Sometimes, however, nothing seems to work. One mother, after hearing examples other mothers had given me for this book said: "I don't have a lot of those wonderfully wide-eyed awesome stories to tell you. Mine are more like, 'Where do you get that from?' in a surprised and shocked how-do-I-deal-with-*this?* vein."

As we talked, it became evident that mothers and fathers of high-need, intense infants and babies often have a difficult time getting support. When these parents tell friends stories about their infant, their friends wonder what they could possibly be doing (wrong) to cause or exacerbate such behaviors. Some friends are sure the parents are exaggerating. The friends often have advice and suggestions they're certain will work. If the problems persist, then the friends think the parents are not following their good advice. As a result, parents of high-need infants and babies often become isolated. They fear judgment or more ill-fated advice.

The mother I was speaking to made the point that she had done all she had read to do, all she believed in her heart she ought to do to calm her baby, but her baby didn't stay calm for long. I reminded her that Dr. Sears did not write his book on the high-need child for just one set of parents. This mother's input reminded me that most of the examples in this book are about children who respond quite easily to respectful parenting techniques. In real life, many families have high-need children. It's important to have examples where respectful parenting does work but is more challenging, taking a great deal more effort on the parents part, and having fewer immediate rewards.

Cindy: With my first daughter, I did all the right things and the result? I had an uncalm baby and intermittent self-doubt. This child was nursing, in a snuggly or a sling on me 24 hours a day. Why? Because if I put her down, she'd be screaming in a second. Not only would she scream, but she'd quickly proceed into turning purple and throwing up if she was let down. Rarely could her father or anyone else comfort her, usually it had to be me. Lots of people offered their advice: "Put her down. It won't take too long, and then she'll get used to it." I just couldn't. The few times I did try, she'd be in such obvious distress, needing to be held, the comfort and security, that I couldn't let her scream. I just didn't have it in me.

At first we thought it was because she had been separated from me right after her birth. She had been born at home, in a quiet loving environment, just as we had planned and dreamed. As soon as she was born I sensed something was wrong. I finally convinced my husband to take her to the hospital.

I was upset because I couldn't go along. I hemorrhaged after her birth, and our midwife said I had to stay put and rest. For the next two days, I wasn't allowed to stay with her and could hold her only occasionally. When she did finally come home, after five days, she still had to be hooked up to oxygen for another eight weeks. She had rapid breathing problems, and the only solution was oxygen, as her lungs had filled up with fluid at birth, her heart valve had closed, and her heart would beat much too quickly. She also had to be on antibiotics, which seemed to really affect her little system. It must have taken us a good year to balance her body after being bombarded by the antibiotics at such a young age.

We kept thinking her unusual need to be held was due to her postbirth trauma and hospital stay...you know, her body being so out of control, being hooked up to machines, deprived of my closeness, the long-term oxygen she had to be on...but over time, she never seemed to get enough. No matter how much holding and rocking I gave her, she still needed more. She would calm down. She just wouldn't stay calmed down for long. I finally figured this is what she brought into this world, and as her mother, I needed to address it as best and lovingly as I could.

So what did I learn from my infant? You can arrange, as much as possible, a mellow home birth. You can be the most devoted, loving parents, holding and understanding your infant's need to be held. You can nurse on demand, lovingly appreciating the nutrition and nurturing you are providing, and you can still have a high-need infant who screams in a way people look at you and say or think, "What is going on with that infant?" or "What is that parent *doing* to that infant?"

I knew I had to keep doing what I was doing. If being loving and understanding was resulting in such vocalizing, then I knew I had to keep reassuring her, with continued closeness and attachment, that I still loved her, that I would be there, and it was okay. It would be okay. I knew that in my head, and mostly in my heart...only sometimes my self-confidence wavered and I wondered . . . It's difficult to do what you believe is right, yet not get the results you know ought to be following . . . Frustrating and scary too . . .

≋

Our daughter cried—no, she screamed, bloodcurdling screams when she was hungry, and that was about every hour and a half, around the clock. So we brought her into our bed for nursing to be easier. Still, in our bed, with me right next to her, when she was ready to nurse, no, when she *needed* to nurse, she'd still cry out in that incredibly intense way. I could respond faster when she was in our bed, so it was easier for all of us.

≋

My mother-in-law visited when my daughter was 10 weeks old. She saw us holding her, seemingly unwilling to put her down, and most of the time walking or rocking her as we held her. It was the only way our daughter seemed to be comfortable—otherwise she'd scream. From the perspective of my mother-in-law, she thought we were being absurd; clearly we were spoiling her. She repeatedly advised, "Just put her down and she'll cry her way through it once or twice and then you'll be past it."

On one of the first days of her visit, we had gone to the supermarket. I had my infant strapped to me in her snuggly as we shopped. When we got back to the car and I began to put her in her car seat, she began to fuss. Ordinarily, I would have spent a few minutes comforting her or seeing if she wanted to nurse before putting her into her car seat. But my mother-in-law said, "Come on, we'll be home in five minutes." So instead of taking the five or ten minutes in the parking lot to comfort and nurse her, I acquiesced and plopped her into her car seat. Within two seconds my daughter had gone from 0 to 100. Crying, screaming, getting purple in the face while screaming, and then throwing up all over herself. At that point I had had enough; I took her out, cleaned her off and comforted her. "Oh, I see," my mother-in-law said, "I hadn't realized . . ."

≋

How do you explain that to someone who hasn't seen it? People just don't want to believe that you can't, as parents, prevent such behavior. But you can't. I quickly learned that I needed to love my daughter with all her unique qualities. I knew, really knew in my heart, she needed our love even more than if she had been a mellow, easier infant. And at times, yes, I was exhausted, and it was hard to maintain such an accepting stance. But thankfully, I could always talk to myself and intellectually understand . . . from somewhere I'd be able to come up with a reserve of love and acceptance to give her.

We knew we had to keep doing what we were doing even if, at that point in time, we weren't getting the results we wanted. Intuitively, and from all we had read, we believed, later in our daughter's life, our continual love, support, and attempts to make her more comfortable (even if the results were for brief periods of time), would be important and healthy for her development. And it's been true. Now, at 5, she's intelligent, sharp, intense, loving, creative—still often a challenge to parent, but also a great kid to be around.

The lesson here is that high-need infants and babies need extra loving and respect so they can become happy, well-adjusted children and adults. This is particularly difficult if you were raised by gruff parents. Your inner tapes will be telling you things like, "Why won't this baby shut up? I'm holding her!" or "I just fed him a half hour ago. He should be asleep by now!" Perhaps your infant needs you to think about her needs rather than your expectations. At times like these, try to remember: your parents didn't know any better. They may have attributed your fussiness to *malicious* attempts on your part to get to them. But you don't have to continue their legacy. You can hear those old, angry tapes and stop yourself from repeating them. Sometimes when you hear the old tapes you can say, "Thank you for sharing," and then go on with what you want to do. By acknowledging your old tapes, you don't get engaged in fighting your personal history, and your energy is free to do something different today. You'll be able to give your child the gifts of love, understanding, and acceptance by embracing your infant heartily, and accepting her needs— even when she challenges you.

Learning Styles

Although this book covers the first three years in a child's life, this chapter was included because it is during these first few crucial years that many of the neurological connections that your child will rely on throughout his life will be made. Recent brain research tells us that 80% of how a child will learn is set by the time the child is 5. By 10, there is almost no more molding or flexibility in learning possible—the child's learning style and learning strategies are largely set. The most you can do at that point is teach your child how to bridge between his learning style and the expectations around him. Bridging can help, but it is a two-step learning process, which will slow down your child's learning. Thus, the first three years is a time in a child's life when his brain cells are firing off stimuli, connections are being made, and certain areas of his brain are being relied on more "naturally" than others. Parents can build on their child's early brain capacity and it's flexibility by stimulating all kinds of connections during these first three years. The more connections that are established at this young age, the better they will serve your child through-out his life.

This is even more important in modern society. It seems that ever since the onset of television and video games, our society is producing a disproportionate number of children who rely on the right side of their brain, which is the visual side, to take in and process information. The other half of the brain (their left side), where logical thinking takes place and the world is understood more in words than with images, seems to be getting downplayed and is not developing as strongly. Ideally, we want to be "whole brained"—able to perceive and process visual information, as well as understanding what is being said to us in longer, sequential type sentences.

Many of our schools' teaching curricula are geared toward left-brained type learning. Our teachers were trained largely in left-brain oriented training programs. Because we seem to be producing more right-brained children and they are going to schools that are used to teaching to a more whole-brain or left-brain oriented student, many children are getting lost in our classrooms. This chapter is an attempt to help you counter some of that societal influence so you can provide your child with a more balanced head start before she begins school.

The main suggestion here is that children need to be talked to. They need to hear explanations where parents take the time to speak in long sentences, using all the sense words. Children need to be read to. They need to hear and learn to understand logical explanations. If they are, parents may be able to stem the tide (so to speak) of this preponderance of children relying on visual stimuli to understand the world around them. A certain amount of how a child will learn is set at birth, but we are finding out that the first few years of life is the time when a brain has the greatest capacity to be flexible, to make new and different connections throughout the brain. You can help your child maximize the areas in which she is comfortable taking in information, retrieving information, and using that information to understand the world around her. As a parent, you can introduce her to a variety of stimuli, not rely on the television, and watch her reactions so you don't bombard her young system. Everything you will be reading about respectful parenting strategies and techniques will help your child.

Strategies

- **Listen carefully, using all of your senses. See, feel, and hear what your child is saying.** You'll get a more accurate and complete message when you use all your senses to listen. This is especially true when you are listening to your preverbal child. You really need all *your* senses to make sense of *his* sounds and actions.

- **Introduce your infant, baby, toddler, and young child to a variety of stimuli and watch your child's reactions.** You want to be introducing your child to a variety of visual, auditory, and tactile things so that all areas of your child's brain are stimulated.

- **Take your cues from your child. Respect your child's limits.** If your child is getting anxious, fidgety, uncomfortable, or experiencing stimulation overload, take your child from the situation and soothe him.

- **Talk to your child using words that encourage your child to see, hear, and feel the world around her.**

- **Read books with your child.** Talk about the pages, make sounds, act like the animals and people on the pages, and use the book as a jumping off point for other fun activities.

The Continuum of Learning

There are a variety of ideas that explain how and why children develop their own particular learning styles. We will be looking at a continuum that goes from right-brain learning, through whole-brain learning, and into left-brain learning styles.

This continuum reflects the right and left hemispheres of a person's brain. The left brain is the area where logical, sequential learning and ideas take place. People who rely on their left brain are linear learners, they learn in logical sequence, and their thinking consists of logical, sequential ideas and words. The more "left-brained" you are, the more this is the case. People who are more comfortable in their left hemisphere think in words, not in images. Left-brained people usually are unable to imagine how things look without seeing them first. For instance, if a person is left-brained and you asked him how he'd like to see his home reconfigured if he had the ability to move walls and change dimensions, he'd be lost. He cannot "imagine" things differently than they are. These kinds of people are rarely artists because they cannot create visual images. They can be engineers and logically take things step by step to create something new, but they would not have a clear vision at the outset of what would be created. This is a "bridging process" for them, going through a two-step process to create something without a clear initial vision.

A person who relies on the right side of his brain tends to be more artistic, creative, and a comparatively nonsequential learner. These people find it easy to create images in their mind. The more right-brained they are, the easier it is for them to create objects based on their imagination. The objects they eventually create do not always look like what they have seen in their mind, but they are some facsimile of their mind's creation. Sometimes as they create, their mind's images change, and the creations themselves change as their images change. The more right-brained you are, the more creative you are. Also, the more right-brained you are, the more you think in pictures. Your pictures may be like photographs or videos, with or without sounds, depending upon where you are along the right-brain continuum.

How your child will learn is in place at birth, to a degree. But you can help your child become as whole-brained as possible, with an ability to be creative and logical, by how you parent.

Hypersensitivity

It seems to be true that the more right-brained you are, the more sensitive you are to all your senses—smell, taste, touch, vision, and auditory stimuli. In extreme situations, children can be hypersensitive. They can hear sounds most other people easily filter out or don't hear at all. Thus, these kids can become very "distractible." They are sometimes labeled Attention Deficit Disorder (ADD) or they are simply right-brained children in a largely left-brained world. For instance, if one of these kids with heightened sensitivities was sitting quietly in "circle time" at day care or preschool, and a dog began barking plaintively down the street, that child, who knew she was supposed to be paying attention, would be distracted by the new sound of the dog. She'd get up to look out the window because the barking was a new stimuli that grabbed her interest. She might even interrupt the current activity and talk enthusiastically about the dog and what might be bothering it, whereas the other children would have remained in their places paying attention to the teacher. That child did not purposely set out to "disrupt" circle time; she was simply following her highly tuned senses and was concerned about the dog.

Some of a right-brained child's other heightened sensitivities come out in complaints of clothes being uncomfortable, seams in socks hurting a child's feet, labels itching, and certain fabrics being so uncomfortable that the child literally can't wear them. If you don't share these kinds of sensitivities, it's easy to think your child is exaggerating, but these highly sensitive children are being real and honest with their complaints. Their sensitivities can be heightened to a hypersensitivity that must be accommodated if they're going to be comfortable and be able to focus on a task at hand.

Many children with these kinds of sensitivities are very bright. They have at least above average intelligence, but they often are challenging to parent and get lost in the classroom because their behavior is distracting to others. They are often in trouble for being disruptive rather than being recognized as very intelligent children with hypersensitivities that they cannot easily control. Because they may be disciplined more often, their self-esteem suffers and they lack confidence in themselves. They know they're different. They know what they should be doing, and they want to please their parents and teachers, but they can't and therefore they feel inadequate.

Using the Strategies

If you parent your child respectfully by going at your child's pace from infancy on, you will not be overly bombarding his system. It is important that you talk to your child because the more you talk logically to your child, explaining things that are happening around him, from a young age, the more your child will be able to follow logical, sequential thoughts and learn in that manner. Instead of lecturing to your child about what you want from her, even when she's young, you can pose logical questions: "What do you think will happen if you pull all your toys out and then don't put them back? How will Mommy feel?" Let your child think about that. Or ask your child to picture Mommy's face after she (the child) has pulled everything off her toy shelves and isn't putting anything back. "What will Mommy's face look like? And then what will Mommy do or say?" That way your child learns how to come to logical conclusions, make some choices, and behave accordingly. This will encourage your child's "whole-brained" development as much as possible.

When you talk to your child, you should use a variety of sense words in your talk and questions: How does that *look* to you? What do you *think* about it? How does that *feel* to you? Can you *see* my reason? How does that *sound* to you? Using different sense words will help your young child expand his mind and be able to feel out situations, look at and perceive situations, hear the whole story before jumping to conclusions, and think things through thoroughly. You want to help your young child use all his senses in any situation instead of getting one image and jumping to a conclusion, because an initial image is only one piece of the whole puzzle of what's occurring around him at any particular point in time. If you are always in a hurry with your child, you will role model jumping to conclusions and acting hastily without thinking things through logically. That will not encourage whole-brained thinking. The ideal is for a child or an adult to be able to think things through and create possibilities in her or his head, to be able to move back and forth across the brain's continuum, depending upon what makes sense in a given situation.

When you read books with your young child, you can point to the object and the word on the page; that way you are encouraging the child's mind to think in words (using the left brain) and images (using the right brain). With babies and toddlers, you don't even have to "read" the stories as they are written; you can talk about the pictures. As your child acquires language skills, you two can make up your own stories about the pictures in addition to the author's words. If you ask your child, "What's happening in this picture?" you are encouraging him to use his imagination and think things through, which is essentially using many areas across the continuum in your child's brain. Every person seems to have one area where he or she is naturally "most comfortable," but that area can have some flexibility.

When you respectfully parent and encourage your child to respond, when you encourage your child to think, to feel, to look at the world around her and to share those thoughts and images with you, you are

---

Encourage Your Child's Full-Brain Capacity

- Use all five sense words when you speak with your child: look, feel, taste, sound, smell.

- Look at books together and talk about the pictures, pointing at them and making sounds, in addition to reading the words.

- When your baby responds in different ways, give explanations of what your baby is doing, e.g., "I can see you're tired of that toy. What do you feel like playing with now? Oh, you've reached for the colorful box. Can you see the pictures on it? A cow goes moo, moo. You're smiling. Do you like that sound? Are you comfortable in my arms playing like this?"

- Introduce your baby to new environments (e.g., the store, a playground, the backyard, a play group) and watch his reactions. Stay close so you can offer comfort and explanations and make sure you don't overload him with stimulation.

- Watch the world through a window and talk about it.

- Ask your child what she wants to know or to point things out to you, then tell her about them.

- Make sure your child gets a variety of stimuli, not just the visual stimuli provided by a television.

encouraging her mind to be flexible—to be comfortable all along the learning continuum. Taking the time to encourage your child's full development will help her tremendously when she is in school. The key here is balanced encouragement rather than stimulation. You want your child's mind to be as flexible as it can be without stressing it to be proficient across the board. A slow pace and long quality time spent with your child are important in this endeavor. Sitting in a chair together, looking out the window, and talking about what you see is a fun way to encourage your child's awareness of the world around her. Encouraging your preverbal child to point at things that interest her and describing them to her in detail can be a fun pastime. *Quantity* stimuli are not the answer—*quality* interactions are. Follow your child's lead and go with it. In this way, you can prevent stimulation overload, discussed in the next section.

Stimulation Overload

In previous chapters, I talked about the importance of listening to your child's needs, even in preverbal stages. If, for instance, your child is affected in crowds, or doesn't do well with multiple errands in a short period of time, you should not force the issue. Instead, you need to take your child into a quieter, less stimulating environment. You want to respond in this way to help your child learn how to judge his limits, which is a logical sequential thinking process. When you respect his limits, he knows he's exercised good judgment. Knowing that helps his self-esteem, and it teaches him not to bombard his senses.

The connection between this and developing a more whole-brained approach lies in the processes of thinking things through; integrating visual, auditory, and tactile stimuli; coming to correct and acceptable conclusions; and presenting them in appropriate ways to people around him. If your child is not naturally far to the right on the brain functioning continuum, and you teach your young child these skills, your child probably will do very well in school because most schools still largely teach in ways that stimulate left-brain thought processes. It is important to note: the extent that you can teach these skills is dependent on where your child was born along the continuum; there is only so much movement and flexibility that can be taught, but you can certainly encourage flexibility within your child's given biological range.

In a speech at Bergen Meadow Elementary School, Evergreen, Colorado, in January 1999, Jeff Freed (coauthor of *Right Brained Children in a Left Brained World* listed in the Other Resources section) presented a powerful reality check for looking at the differences between growing up today and growing up in less complex times. In the 1950s, most families lived in one or two houses over a 20- or 30-year period. They did not move around the country adjusting to different climates, cultures, and neighborhoods. Most babies were stay-at-home babies with a stay-at-home mom. Babies were not brought out in public as much as they are today. They were not usually brought to a day care center for 8 to 10 hours a day. They were not exposed to a group of other children and a variety of caregivers before kindergarten. Children had fewer toys. Back then, there were a few television stations, and they weren't on 24 hours a day. Television shows were filmed at a slower pace—think of *Gunsmoke* vs. *NYPD Blue*—even the camera movements were simpler then. The commercials were lower key. Babies were not exposed to black-and-white shapes and patterns over their cribs as infants. They did not have complex activity boards hanging in their cribs. Parents read to them from simple books without sounds. The visual and auditory stimuli in their environment was far less than a baby's stimuli today.

Can you see how today's quantity of stimuli might feel like a bombardment to a young, unexposed infant, baby, or toddler? Can you see how important it is to help that child feel comfortable and understand the world around him? Can you see how important your roles as parent/translator/guide can be? Can you see where you need to slow down the stimuli, explain it so your baby has an understanding, so your baby is not forcing and straining his own brain to make whatever sense he can from all that is coming at him? Can you hear your baby's cries of "enough, slow it down," and can you respect those cries? Can you see how by respecting your baby's cries and early verbal messages, that you are indeed teaching the baby to respect himself and his own limits?

When you are under stress as an adult—too much is coming at you at work, during your commute, or at home—all you want to do is slow down the action, figure it out, and take it one step at a time. But the pace doesn't slow down, and your boss hands you yet another project to pack into your busy day. All you want to do is scream, retreat, or stop the world. But you don't, because you're an adult. You cope as best as you can.

Well, your child needs role modeling on how to cope. Your child needs you to slow down the action, let him breathe, and take it all in slowly. Your child needs to digest the information coming at him. If you give your child the gift of time, the gift of being a gentle guide and patient translator, you'll be giving your child the gift of having as flexible an area of functioning in his brain as possible. You'll be encouraging your child to do well with what he takes on, to know his limits, and not take on too much. Your child will have a better chance in school and in life.

One woman I worked with couldn't understand why her young baby did not "appreciate" all the toys he had been given. She said, "He only likes to hold one thing, like all day. I try and give him other toys, because he has to be bored with that one rattle, but he cries when I take that day's favorite thing from him."

I asked her if she could identify all her assumptions in what she had just said. She seemed confused at first, but then made the following list: (1) her baby didn't "appreciate" all his toys; (2) there was something wrong with only wanting one thing; (3) he *had* to be bored with one thing; (4) he *should* take what she was offering; and (5) she knew how to play better than he did.

She laughed nervously as she said the last assumption. I reassured her that she was doing very well by being able to identify her assumptions. I then asked her whose assumptions they were. She thought they were the kind of messages she had received as a child: "They were probably my parents' assumptions."

I asked her what else her child might be telling her if her parents' assumptions were inaccurate. She came out with, "He likes things simple. He's not ready for more." We both agreed that might be his message. Her "assignment" that week was to follow his simple lead more and see where it went.

The next week, she came in with a sheepish grin. "I tried it. Boy, what a difference. We had such a peaceful week and he does like playing, but he doesn't like a lot of stuff. He seemed to drift off to sleep more easily. A couple of times I felt myself getting bored, but I tried to remind myself that I'm supposed to be there for him, not him for me. When I could realize that I was the bored one, not him, I could usually refocus my attention." We talked about being in awe and sharing his awe as a way of warding off her boredom. She found that helped, too.

The Joy of Learning

Watching your child learn can be an awesome experience when you truly appreciate your child's efforts. Every second of every waking minute in your young child's life is full of stimuli and learning. Your infant is continuously taking in stimuli through her ears, her eyes, and her fingers. There are also new smells and tastes to take in. Children need help categorizing, understanding, and making sense of this new and multifaceted world they are encountering. It is your job as parent to caringly guide your child through this stimulating process. You are the translator. You are their Rock of Gibralter they can reconnect with for comfort, for understanding. The more you are available when they need you, the safer their world seems. The safer their world seems, the more adventurous and independent they can become. They will go experience the world and bring their questions back to you. They will respect your knowledge and wisdom and use it in their decisions. Their decisionmaking will take place using the skills they acquired in their well-developed brain. What a wonderful pattern to establish in infancy and take to adulthood.

6

Learning with Your Baby

I t is difficult to impose a distinct time delineation between infancy and babyhood. Where does one stop and the next stage of development begin? When it seems to you that your infant has turned a corner, becoming significantly more responsive and social, then she has left infancy and become a "baby." In rereading a daily journal I wrote about my own child, I found the following entries that clarified my thinking. The first was written when my son was 1 week shy of 3 months: "Today I realized you definitely don't look like an infant anymore. You are so alert and responsive. I can see your brain going. Your disposition remains light and sunny." By the end of that month I wrote, "What a month. Every day, every hour, every minute is so full of new things ... You communicate your needs so well, like coming off my breast repeatedly or raising your hands up straight when you need burping. You squeal with delight. Your smile lights up your face and mine. One day late in the month, you looked at me, smiled, and lifted your right eyebrow. What a face! You've definitely changed this month from an infant to a baby..."

Being a "baby" starts right after infancy and continues until your child is beginning to toddle around. Once your baby begins toddling, there's a whole new world of stimuli and learning going on. Some babies begin toddling at 9 months, others wait till they're 18 months or older. The ages can vary quite a bit, but it's during this stage that you'll begin to get clues about the pace your baby will be using to deal with life. His frustration level begins to be apparent. You can see evidence of how he will tolerate discomfort. You can learn what makes him laugh. He'll show you his level of curiosity. You'll begin to see how he moves his body and his own particular brand of grace. He'll even begin to tell you he wants things or wants to know about things. You have to watch carefully to pick up the nuances that are essential in deciphering your baby's emerging character development.

Strategies

- **Focus on your child.**
- **Slow down.**
- **Listen carefully, using all of your senses.**
- **Be spontaneous.**
- **Begin reading to your baby.**
- **Talk with your baby.**

Communicating with Your Baby

The latest research on infant and early development shows babies are capable of a lot more than we previously thought. For instance, at a few months old they are responsive to different language stimuli. I'm sure some overly anxious parents will run out, purchase, and play language tapes while their baby is sleeping. That is probably overdoing it. But recognizing your baby is an intelligent small human being, taking in a lot more than you may think, can remind you to follow your baby's lead, build on her interest, respond to her curiosity, and go at her pace.

You can encourage your baby's sounds by making the same intonations back to her. If your baby says, "ba," you can say "ba" back. Before you try and get your baby to say a real English word, encourage her in her own language. After saying "ba" a few times together, you could go on to say a few familiar words that have a "ba" sound, like *ball, baby, banana,* or stretch it to *book.* But always repeat your baby's sounds first so she feels "heard" and then suggest yours. Watch your baby's face light up with glee as she hears you repeat her sounds. When you do that, you're validating her reality, and that feels good to any human being at any age.

The more you talk with your baby, the faster your baby will catch on to language and be making all kinds of sounds on his own. When you interact with your baby, in ways that show you're as interested in his form of "conversations" as you would be with any interesting, engaging human being, you'll be encouraging his social and emotional development. It's fun to challenge yourself and work really hard if necessary to tell what he means from his gestures and tone of voice. In other words, when your baby jabbers at you, jabber back in his language. It's fun for both of you. On an intuitive level, your baby will feel understood, safe, and good. You can have full jabber conversations or intersperse real words and sentences in there. You'll be playing, building your child's self-esteem, and teaching him valuable early language skills in addition to the social skills of give and take.

Stimulating Your Baby

Babies want to learn. They are hungry for information and stimulation (when they're not sleeping). Babies are self-motivated little beings. They only seem to lose motivation when they aren't encouraged. Traditionally, it was thought that small babies should be kept at home, but today parents are encouraged to take their babies with them, to stimulate them by exposing them to different places and things. When they learn, from a young age, that the world is full of different stimuli while they have the safety and comfort of Mommy and Daddy, they may be less timid and therefore more self-assured about venturing out and doing things when they're older.

Parents need to respect their baby's individual ability to take in stimuli. If your baby seems to have a low tolerance for stimulation or noise, then you need to respond by cutting down the amount of stimulation your baby is exposed to. It's a balancing act of enough stimulation and enough rest, quiet time, and individual attention. When a baby's needs are not addressed repeatedly, and the baby is trying to tell the parents "I've had enough," the baby will get more upset. Over time, the baby may associate noise and activity with discomfort. This could lead the baby to dislike and withdraw from noise and people later in life, recalling on an unconscious level his initial discomfort and trying to alleviate that early unresolved discomfort and pain.

There isn't a "correct" mixture for all babies. But if you follow your baby's lead and respect the cues you get, you'll find the "correct" mixture for *your* baby. Babies' comfort levels also change over time, depending on their previous experiences, what they've learned about the world around them, and how they're feeling at any given moment. As a parent, you need to be on your toes to respond to today's "ideal" mixture with spontaneity and appreciation.

The most common cue your baby will give you when she has had enough (or too much) is a cry of discomfort. If your baby's crying stops when you take her out of the immediate environment to a place where you can soothe and comfort her, you know you've reached your baby's limit, and your baby needs less of what was happening. Sometimes your baby can be adversely affected by the people around her, sometimes by the noise, sometimes by the temperature, sometimes by smells. Your child's discomfort can also stem from internal factors like fatigue or hunger. If you do encounter crying on your first few excursions, try to vary the type of setting and the time of day before giving up and staying home.

Parents who expect too much, too soon, can build in problems for their babies, because their babies cannot perform to their parents' expectations and they can sense their parent's disappointment. They can interpret their parent's disappointment as their own personal failure. Parents who expect too little can also inadvertently build in problems for their children by not stimulating them enough. Lack of stimulation and inadequate nurturing can lead to developmental delays and emotional problems as these babies grow up. We have seen these problems in children who have been adopted in foreign countries from orphanages where they did not receive adequate nurturing or holding during infancy, and in children who have been passed from foster home to foster home, never staying long enough to get the attention, love, and understanding they need. As a result, these children sometimes have a great deal of trouble "bonding" or maintaining close relationships. There is a term, *attachment disorder,* which encompasses extreme reactions to not enough closeness in early life and what happens to a child later on. At either extreme, getting too much stimulation or not getting enough, a baby's self-esteem can be damaged and his mental and emotional processes can be affected.

A baby isn't able to make sense out of all the things he is experiencing, but his little computer brain is soaking up the stimuli every time he turns and observes another angle in his world. He will process some of the stored information later, when he has more building blocks and experiences to match with previous experiences. Still other information will remain lodged in his unconscious mind, affecting his behavior and emotions in years to come in ways he himself won't understand.

Keeping Your Baby Entertained

Strategies

- **Play.** Sounds simple—but it can be difficult to leave your adult responsibilities and thoughts aside and get down on the floor and play, following your child's lead. This is an activity that you can learn from your child (in case you've forgotten how to play or set it aside as being too immature for you). Playing with soft blocks for 30 minutes is different than playing a couple of holes of golf. Kid play is much freer than adult play. You'll need to be spontaneous and leave your adult agenda aside if you're going to share a respectful play time with your small child.

- **Follow your child's lead whenever possible, rather than imposing your own agenda.**

- **Switch to being in awe with your baby if you begin to feel bored.** Rediscover the world through his eyes rather than trying to change to a new activity when your baby is still satisfied and engaged with what he is doing.

Sometimes while parents are playing with their baby, they forget to follow their baby's lead. For instance, one baby was watching fascinatingly as her mother was holding and showing her a small, stuffed-animal rocking horse. Finally, the baby reached for it, grabbed it, and was looking at it, when the mother said, "Jenny, look what else Mommy has for you." What hidden messages are in that mother's action? The mother meant well; she was just showing Jenny another toy. But Jenny was still involved and had just engaged with the first toy. Unconsciously is Jenny being told to hurry up with things? Or that she takes too long at things? That she should be interested in the same things others are? That she should put her interests aside? All those messages are unconsciously being received, along with, "Stop what you're doing and look at this (this thing I'm showing you)," or, 'I'm more important than you." Such messages discount the baby's interests.

I think parents do that kind of thing out of their own boredom. They're tired of looking at the (in this case) stuffed-animal rocking horse; they're ready for another toy. But was their baby? Whose needs and interests are they there to stimulate? Their own or their baby's? You may say both, and that's true. If a parent is bored, he won't be a good play companion with his baby. But if the parent's needs usually come first, then they're forgetting to pace their baby and not respecting their baby's natural curiosity or intellectual functioning.

The solution in respectful parenting terms is to get interested in your baby's interest. Of course you may tire of a toy before your baby, but then stop looking at the toy as the object of stimulation and shift your focus to your baby and how she's interacting with the toy. What is your child discovering? Shapes? Textures? Colors? Movements? Observing your child's interactions with things and her awe will keep your interest a lot longer than any toy will.

Baby Games

- Build a little tower of soft blocks or toys and let her knock it down or move it around.
- Lay her under a tripod with hanging toys and help her make them move, sharing in her delight.
- Converse with her in a mixture of baby and adult speech.
- Comment on what your baby is doing, giving her a running description of her playful accomplishments.
- Find things to giggle about: a feather on the skin, a block falling off the top of a pile, a tickle, an animal at the zoo.
- Put things in a container and let your baby "help." Transfer small play items or shapes from one container to another.
- Play on drums to music, using pots, pans, wooden spoons, chopsticks, and other kitchen utensils.
- Dance around the room with your baby safely in your arms.
- Big pop-together beads can be fun for beginning to teach colors and manual dexterity.

Watch your baby learn, discover, enjoy, and see how she fills her knowledge cup. Look for cues that tell you she's ready for something new. Let her ask in her own way before you offer or take over and introduce something new. Ideally, you want your child to enjoy exploring and learning about new things as much as possible. You could be discouraging just such a thoughtful process by presenting too many toys in too short a time. Again, follow your baby's lead by presenting stimulating things at your baby's pace, not yours.

The Benefits of Being in Awe

Being in awe with your child will bring you a rich source of pure joy and excitement. As an adult, you often wear blinders that leave you oblivious to a lot of what's happening around you. The end result: like a horse on a racetrack, you function with the tasks at hand, but ignore the beauty and richness of the world around you. Your baby's enthusiastic eyes can break through your blinders, bringing you endless hours of wonder and awe.

Being in awe of your children will open your senses to being in awe with them, which in turn will expose you to endless, simple pure pleasures of experiencing the world through their senses. You'll be able to communicate with them and truly be there with them, experiencing what they are experiencing, appreciating their discoveries, their accomplishments, and feeling as warm and excited inside as they do.

You can give them such incredible gifts by understanding and appreciating their discoveries. They will be giving you the incredible gift of rekindling your innocent appreciation of the world and everything that catches their eye. Perhaps you'll even notice things you've ignored or never seen before and be able to bring it to their attention if they haven't noticed it first. Being in awe will (re)awaken your senses. What better basis for establishing a respectful relationship can there be?

Carl: My baby has this plastic rattle with a piece that spins on it. He likes the rattle a lot. I used to show him how the piece spun by taking my index finger and making it move. He'd stare in complete fascination as the little wheel spun. One day recently, I saw him crawling toward the rattle on the floor, pick it up, and actually take his tiny index finger and twirl the spinner. He had the most serious look on his face as he watched the part spin. As it slowed, he made it go again, watching seriously until I came up, interrupting his interactions by congratulating him. I was so excited to see him doing that all on his own. He even used the same finger I did to spin the thing. Incredible!

Laurel: When our baby was about 6 months old, my husband bought one of those trailers for babies that hooks onto a bicycle. It's incredible to see this little baby get very excited each time he sees his dad take out the trailer. He knows he's going, too. Actually, I don't know which one is more excited, my son or my husband. My husband can't get the thing attached fast enough. And my son waves his arms as if to say, "Hurry up, where's my helmet? Let's go." As they drive off, I can see their faces, beaming with delight. I love seeing them like that.

Bonnie: Sometimes the associations my daughter makes just amaze me. She has this beautiful fish mobile in her room made out of bright, woven ribbons. She loves to see them "swim" when we blow on them. Recently, we went to visit my parents who have a real fish aquarium in their house. I said, "Oh look, fish" to her, and she immediately toddled over and blew at the fish tank. My mother didn't understand that at all until I told her about the mobile. When we got home and my mother called us, I asked my daughter if she wanted to talk to her and she got on the phone and immediately blew into the phone. Her association was just amazing.

Safety Concerns

When a baby's curiosity has taken her to places and things you would rather not have her encounter, it's important to remember that her curiosity is capable of motivating her to wander and reach delicate, favorite, breakable, nonreplaceable, and dangerous things, but she's still a baby and doesn't deserve blame or shame for interfering with something she "should know better about." Instead, you as the parent should know better than to leave it within your baby's reach. It's your responsibility to "know better," not your baby's.

Instead of an old-fashioned admonishment or spanking, stop her movement with a gentle hug/hold, followed by an explanation she can use effectively and respectfully: "I can see you're curious, but Daddy knows that's dangerous for you. I'm sorry it's within your reach. Let me take that out of your hands so you're safe." Or you could say, "There now, let's wait a second while I help you," followed by an explanation. Either is a loving way to set a limit with your baby, and it can calm your fears about a favorite object being broken.

Babies won't instill anger in you if you remember that they're naturally curious little human beings. They want to explore everything that invites them by simply being in their world. You might comfort yourself by knowing that the more curious they are, the more intelligent they are. Their interest needs to be stimulated, not curbed. This will be safe for your baby if you childproof your house. You'll probably need to rechildproof your house as your child grows and is able to reach different levels. Otherwise you'll find yourself lunging to save precious objects from your baby's curious hands and to save your baby from accidents with heavy, breakable, or otherwise dangerous objects.

You may find yourself wanting to construct shelves around your house about five feet off the floor so you have access to things you want and your baby stays safe. An easier solution is cabinet and drawer latches. There's always the "scarcity model" of knickknacks: put them away until your child is old enough to have developed better dexterity and can handle them carefully. It makes life easier and more relaxing.

By employing these simple safety procedures, you'll know that when your baby grabs for an object, it's something he can handle. You won't be sitting on the edge of your seat, watching every move he makes. He's free to roam and explore. You might leave a kitchen cabinet unlatched and full of light, unbreakable plastic containers. This may prove to be your baby's favorite thing . . . crawling to that cabinet, opening the door, and pulling every plastic container and lid out of the cabinet until it's completely empty. Babies who enjoy doing that usually smile proudly at their parents as they sit amidst the array of containers strewn around the kitchen floor. It looks like absolute glee on their faces as they behold their ability to empty the entire cabinet. Maybe it's a little bit of role modeling, doing what they see Mommy and Daddy doing.

The positive side is that you get to watch how babies' minds work and what triggers their interests and subsequent actions. It can be fascinating and such fun to watch a baby play and explore!

What the Parents Say

Sarah: When our baby was 3 ½ months old, my husband and I left him with my parents for a few hours while we went out to dinner. When we came back, my parents were chuckling. I asked them why. They said that our baby had spent the better part of the first two hours entertaining them. They had wanted to watch a program on TV, so they had propped him in his infant seat facing them. They had been talking and interacting with him, but when the program began, they started to ignore him. He began with my mother, staring at her intensely until she felt his gaze. When she looked at him, he started smiling. Then he turned his gaze to my father. Apparently, my mother's attention hadn't been enough. He wanted both of them watching him. My father, like my mother, felt his gaze and looked down at him. He, too, got a big smile. Well, my son played that game over and over, graduating from a smile to a giggle with both of them. They ended up taping the program and playing his game for a long time.

John: It's difficult to say, but I know my wife was more enthralled with our baby than I was when he was tiny. I think it was his first winter, so my son would have been about 10 months old when I saw him do something that just struck me, and probably changed our relationship quite a bit. It certainly changed the way I saw him. . . . I mean, this kid had a definite sense of humor. I was sitting opposite him as he was maneuvering pieces of banana from his high chair tray into his mouth. He kind of cooed and smiled as he ate. Then, out of the blue, he picked up a piece and held it out toward me, as if he was going to share. Well, my heart just melted. He was sharing all on his own. He wanted to share with me, his daddy. So I, of course, reached out to take the banana he was offering. As I was about to take it, he pulled his hand back quickly and smiled, his eyes sparkling. At first I wasn't sure if he had changed his mind about sharing, but when he did it again, I realized: it wasn't that he didn't want to share or had changed his mind. No, this kid was teasing me. Here was my son, 10 months old, and he had gotten me. I looked at him with more respect and awe that day, realizing he was indeed becoming his own little person. And what a cutie.

Linda: You can just see them learning sometimes. It's fascinating. Like the morning my daughter maneuvered herself over to the coffee table, pulled herself up holding onto it, then pulled the drawer open, grabbed out the boxes full of coasters and happily spilled the coasters all over the floor. What glee and accomplishment were reflected on her face. I loved seeing her mind connect with her body and do all that.

Annie: I'm really in the throes of deciding how much you push them to grow and how much you accept their messages. I started an exercise class 2 or 3 weeks ago, and my 10-month-old daughter is having a hard time adjusting to the on-site babysitter. The first few times she cried so much, the woman in charge came and got me after ten minutes. I had asked her to get me if she was still crying after 10 minutes. The second week she did better, crying intermittently throughout the hour, but the rest of the day she was so clingy, she didn't want me out of her sight. This week, she's doing a little better, but she's beginning to wake up more at night (although she had actually started doing that before I began the exercise class). I'm trying to figure out if I should just give up on the idea of exercising for a while. I'm not sure. There's steady improvement, but.... I hate to see her upset. The last time I picked her up she had fallen asleep in the swing, but her face didn't look peaceful, she looked upset in her sleep, which I've seen every once in a while, but not often...I wonder...

This mother and I talked for a while and decided that before she gave up, there were two things she could try: leaving her daughter for less than the hour, since she seemed to be doing fine 30 minutes or so, and gradually leaving her a little longer until Mom could take the whole class. The second thing she was going to try was talking to her daughter about how important the class was to her and showing her some of what she'd be doing while she was away from her. That way, the mother would be sharing the process and reasons why she was leaving her daughter for an hour, three days a week. When I ran into this woman a few months later, she told me that she had tried both things we had talked about and they had worked really well.

Toddler Lessons

New Skills

The beginning of toddlerhood can vary by as much as one year. Some babies walk before they crawl, others run before they walk. Whenever they begin, walking is a great accomplishment for a baby. You can see the delight all over their faces. In fact, sometimes it looks like the toddler's whole body is smiling with pride and excitement. Toddlers have a whole new view of their world because they are standing and their eyes can see things from a new perspective. It's time to childproof differently because your child can walk and climb.

It may be easier for older babies to begin to "toddle," because they may be more prepared emotionally and intellectually for the consequences of walking: it's farther to fall, the bumps hurt more, and their legs can carry them places they don't belong (ledges, precipices, or anywhere away from Mommy and Daddy). Right after walking comes more proficient climbing, with its share of ups and downs. A 9-month-old really hasn't experienced the world and its limits as much as a 12-, 14-, or even 18-month-old.

Parents need to watch toddlers carefully. Their freedom is heady, and they usually don't have a firmly entrenched sense of danger, limits, space, distance, or fear. When toddlers exhibit pure excitement and pride in themselves, those feelings are pure for them, because they don't have the socialized sense of fear and limits that parents need to provide. It's a balancing act, to provide necessary physical limits without taking too much away from their newfound sense of confidence, self-esteem, and adventure. How do you learn to say, "Gee, that's a little dangerous to be walking toward those stairs right now. I'm not sure you're ready to safely navigate them—let me help you learn," rather than, "Oh, my God, don't go near those—you could fall and crack your head open!"

How do you acknowledge that your child has just entered another developmental period and yet keep in mind that your toddling child is still a baby? His maturity and life experience hasn't changed, just his motor skills. Once you see your child motoring around on his own legs rather than crawling, it's so easy to forget that your child is still basically a nubile, inexperienced little human being who needs just as much love, understanding, respect, and support he needed the day before he started walking. In fact, maybe more, because his world has gotten instantly bigger and taller as his visual perspective has changed with his newfound physical talents.

His world has exploded wide open, leaving him excited about exploring all he can reach now that he's standing upright. Your world has become infinitely more scary as you can see imminent perils and dangers in his path, of which he is completely unaware. The solution? One woman humorously suggested head-to-toe padding and a helmet. Your goal is to instill caution without undue fear, encouragement without overestimating his physical abilities, and lots of loving attention.

One child I know skipped walking and took off running. He had been crawling for a few months. One day, he pulled himself to a standing position by hanging onto a lawn chair, looked around, and then took off running after his two older brothers who were playing basketball on the street. He had an unsteady, seemingly about-to-fall-over gait. But he was running. I ran inside to tell his mother, who came out laughing at the sight. I was sure he must have been walking for a few weeks and I had never seen it, but no, she said, this was it: his transition from crawling straight to running—no need to walk for him. Do you think it was any coincidence that that little boy started running track when he was 9 years old?

Setting Limits

Toddlers often operate from their enthusiasm and curiosity. It is fascinating to watch a group of toddlers and see which ones have no sense of restraint or personal danger while others seem to instinctively know certain things are not to be done, as tempting as they may look. Others are very clingy to their parents and wouldn't venture more than a few feet away. When you observe this, you realize how unique children are even at this young age and how much "personality" each little toddler possesses. Some toddlers are perfectly content to just sit on mom's lap watching other children begin to walk around a room, bouncing off each other as they perfect their balance. Others are in the lead, careening around with other children following behind.

It's important to begin setting reasonable limits that take into account your own child's personality—how much freedom is safe for your child. Telling your child once will not be enough at this stage. Sometime parents lose their tempers with toddlers because they expect that if they've told their child to stay off the table once, their child should listen. But then they find them climbing on it and looking down through the clear glass to their toys underneath. A parent could come over, sweep the child up into his arms and say angrily, "I heard your mother tell you not to climb on that table, now what's the matter with you. You're going to have to go to your room for the rest of the evening because you don't listen!"

This would be an unnecessary overreaction. If your child could talk and felt safe enough to respond, she might say, "But I never saw my toys from up above, I wanted to see what they looked like through the table," an innocent and curious perspective. So often, toddlers are just following their brain's questions and curiosity. They don't have the ability of forethought, they can't think through a situation before they act and look at all the ramifications. It's up to parents to teach them how to think things through: "Climbing on the glass table does allow you to see your toys underneath. But it's also dangerous, because the glass can break and hurt you. Tables are not for climbing. We go to the park for climbing. Thank you for listening."

Strategies

- **Focus on your child's growing world.**

- **Teach your child to slow down and learn about new things.**

- **Childproof your house to your child's new height.**

- **Play, but begin teaching more and explaining more complex concepts like safety and thinking before doing.**

- **Listen with the idea that you're willing to change or compromise your ideas if your child suggests something you hadn't considered.**

- **When you're feeling stuck and you can't think of how to handle a situation in a respectful way,** ask yourself, "What do I, (fill in your name), as a ___-year-old adult on (today's date, including the year) want to do?" By reminding yourself of your age and today's date, including the year, you'll be more likely to access that mature, healthy, creative part of yourself.

- **As you begin to set limits, remember that repetition is the key.** Once is seldom enough.

Using The Strategies

When your toddler is doing something you asked her not to, it is time to calmly take her in your arms and explain to her what you want her to refrain from doing, why you want that (i.e., for her safety, what might happen), and interject with questions and ask her if she understands. Toddlers, in spite of their own limited vocabulary, understand much more than they speak, and reasoning *can* work.

After that conversation, it's important to keep watching carefully to make sure your toddler doesn't forget. If she repeats the action, remind her, "Remember, no climbing on the table. I want you to be safe." If your child doesn't listen as you tell her and she is about to climb again, and she continues to climb, then you can give her a reasonable consequence: "I guess we'll have to give you and the living room a time-out because you can't seem to remember about not climbing. We'll just stay away from the room for a while and see if you can remember better in 15 minutes. We'll leave everything in its time-out while you play someplace else and think about remembering better about glass tables being tables and not climbing structures."

With these kinds of explanations, you are beginning to lead your child through a process they need to learn—thinking things through to their end before acting. This is a difficult lesson to learn. Adults sometimes have trouble thinking things through before acting. Parents need to be patient with their toddlers. But, the more you do this with a toddler, the less frustrating the next stage—the terrific twos—will be, because your child will be used to looking at situations and figuring them out rather than being instantly frustrated with them. Your harder parental work during this toddler stage sets the groundwork for easier stages to come.

Let's look at another scenario: Let's see how something that previously was high enough to be out of reach can become a curiosity, a desire, and then a mess, and how you should react. A toddler climbs on a couch, reaches for a pretty red plate, which drops and breaks. From the toddler's perspective, she is delighted with her new ability to climb, she is looking at a plate that she's been looking at, maybe even been held up to look at and touch for the pretty color. When the plate falls and makes a big noise, the toddler begins to cry. Mom hears her daughter crying in the living room and runs in to see what's wrong. She sees her daughter on the couch, looking over the side at all the pieces on the floor.

That's how easy a curious desire becomes a big mess. Mom has a choice about how to react—angrily or time to teach a valuable lesson. "Oh, that's too bad. I liked that plate a lot. I guess I should have put it away when you started climbing around. Did you want to see it up close like when I'd hold you to look at it?"

Child nods.

"I can understand that. It was pretty. You know what honey? Sometimes when you want to see things and they aren't your toys, you need to come and get me first to help. Especially things that are heavy or that can break. Did you know that could break into so many pieces?"

"No."

"I didn't think so. Now you've learned. That was sad, huh?

Child nods tearfully again.

"You know how sometimes Mommy has you help clean up? Well, this time I just want you to watch because these kinds of pieces can cut you. You can help carry over the dust pan and I'll get the broom, come on."

An old style parent would say something like, "Oh, no! I can't believe you broke my plate! What were you doing over there? Why did you touch it? Don't you know better than to touch my things?"

This second reaction instills shame and blame in your child. It is not good for your child's self-esteem and it doesn't have the parent taking any responsibility for her part in the situation. There is nothing wrong with curiosity, a child just needs to learn how to deal with her curiosity so it doesn't lead to an unwanted consequence. A child needs curiosity to learn. You don't want to squelch curiosity at a young age, you want to teach your toddler how to begin to manage their curiosity.

Wants vs. Needs

A different but overlapping area to begin teaching your toddler is the difference between wants and needs. This is another one of those life-long lessons that can begin in "toddlerhood." Earlier in this book, I talked about not being able to spoil an infant or a baby because they only had needs, not wants, and addressing needs immediately. Well, this is not true anymore. Toddlers, whose world has expanded dramatically due to their higher and larger visibility, have gone from *needing* more food to *wanting* something that looks interesting but may not be a toy.

This is another one of those difficult lessons in life, the difference between needs and wants and the artful game of waiting for the appropriate time. People of all ages are very used to instant gratification or "I want what I want when I want it." You may be able to relate. If your credit card comes in with you owing more than you can pay, then you probably haven't learned this lesson very well. Let's see if you can learn, with your toddler, that sometimes you have to wait.

Let's say you ask your toddler what he wants to eat and he happily responds, "Ice cream."

"Now there is an interesting idea. Ice cream for breakfast. I'm sorry. I should have given you a choice of cereal or eggs because that's what I meant for you to choose from. Would you like cereal or eggs for breakfast."

"Ice cream, ice cream. I want ice cream!"

"I know you *want* ice cream but you *need* to eat something better for breakfast so you can play all you want today. Again, your choices are eggs or cereal. Which do you want, because ice cream is not an option. "

"Egg."

"Thanks. You've got it. I'll fix an egg for you."

In this conversation, the parent has apologized for leaving the choice too open-ended and has offered acceptable choices with an explanation of why the child can't have his desire—ice cream. The child will feel respected because his parent did take his choice seriously, but there was a good explanation of why that was not possible. These kinds of "lessons" are instrumental for your toddler to learn the difference between "I want" and "I need." This is another way you can help your child prepare for later developmental stages. The better your child learns the differences between needs and wants, and that wants often wait or may never happen, the easier your child will experience being 2, 3, 4 years, and beyond.

What the Parents Say

Linda: I think it was when my daughter was about 18 months old that I started realizing what a cool sense of humor she had. One day we were gardening, and bees kept coming around. We were in the vegetable garden and seemed to be in the bees' direct route to the flowers beyond. She was getting scared of the bees and I thought we might have to go inside. Instead, I took some time, gathered her in my arms, and talked to her about bees: how they weren't there to bother or hurt us, they just wanted to get to the flowers so they could make their honey. I tried to reassure her that they wouldn't hurt us if we didn't hurt them.

I could tell she felt better and when asked she said yes, she did want to stay and garden some more. A little while later, another bee went flying right by her head, and she pulled herself back a little and said, "Excuse me, bee!" I was so amazed. Thinking about it later, her response showed such a sharp sense of humor, plus she must have really understood and been reassured by what I told her . . . Pretty incredible!

≈

I think my daughter was about the same age when I noticed how responsive she was to other children, especially babies. Like in a mall: if we were walking along and she heard a baby crying, she'd say something like, "There's a baby crying. He needs his Mommy," or "He needs to nurse." Sometimes if we could see the baby and his or her mother was ignoring him, she'd ask, "Why isn't that Mommy holding (or nursing) the baby? He's crying." She would be so concerned. I'd try to explain that not all mothers raise their children the same way I was raising her, and then she'd be even more confused and concerned.

I had trouble explaining why, if she asked for more of an explanation, because I don't know why all Moms don't respond quickly when their babies cry. But I do know that how my husband and I parent is unfortunately in the minority. I'm reminded of that most times we're in public places and each time we go see our extended families.

Her compassion for others still impresses me. I guess it's because she's been responded to so much, her needs have always been addressed, that's all she knows...role modeling, huh? It seems to go a long way.

When we go see relatives who parent differently, who yell at their kids, or spank their kids, or whose kids get told they're "bad" and "in trouble," my daughter just stands back, hangs close to me, and watches. They think we're "just lucky" to have such a mellow kid. They also think some of our parenting ideas are at least a little weird. Actually, I think *they* think we're really out there. They don't associate how we parent, so gently and responsively to her needs and desires, as a reason why we have such an easy mellow little girl. It's not luck at all. She is shown love freely. We talk about her in positive terms, she gets praised a lot. And she herself is loving.

When my daughter started toddling, a whole new world opened up to her and to me. I had to often remember to ignore my first instinct. For instance, if we were walking along and I wanted to get someplace, but she had noticed an ant, and she wanted to stop and watch it move, my first instinct could be to brush her off and say, "Yeah, that's an ant." But if I ignored that, and crouched down with her, we'd have just the greatest time watching that ant, how he moved, what he could carry, and then we'd notice more ants and watch them too. We'd talk about them and watch them ... maybe even recount the incident to Daddy that night. If I hadn't ignored my first "so what?" response, I would have missed out on seeing the ants...And when is the last time I had *seen* ants?

Bonnie: Sometimes it seems a little harder as my daughter gets older. I have to remember to look at things differently, and there's more things to look at as she's more active and asserts herself. Like when she wants to read a book for the hundredth time. And of course, at 13 months, usually if she wants to read a book, it involves Mommy reading it to her.

At those times, I have to remember consciously it's her task, her job of childhood to enjoy the familiarity she feels with a favorite book. That's what kids her age do naturally. But I also have to honor my needs. And how can I always do that and still be there for her? I reframe the situation, enjoy her enjoyment, and get my needs met, not from the hundredth reading of her current favorite book, but from her, her little spirit as she sits there on my lap, cuddling as I read to her. That's pretty special. Enough to make up for the perceived boredom of a hundredth reading.

～

Sometimes, when my 13-month-old daughter needs my attention and I need a break, I try to find something that will interest her, like a book, or crayons and paper. I tell her she's resourceful and resilient, that I'm just going to take a break for a few minutes and then come back to her. I let her know where I'm going and she can call me if she really needs me. I try to let her know she'll be fine. She usually responds really well when I leave, because she's focused on something that doesn't involve me. Then I run and make a quick phone call to a friend just for the adult conversation. I can go back to her refreshed and start playing with her again. It just takes a few minutes, but it's so important to me and to her. I want to role model taking care of myself so she doesn't grow up being self-sacrificing.

Sarah: When my son was about 21 months old and still rather nonverbal, I saw him exhibit such compassion with one of his day care buddies, I was really touched. We had just arrived at day care and one of his teachers was standing outside his room, holding one of the other little boys he often played with (or near). The other little boy (we'll call him David) was crying hard. My son indicated by pointing and saying "Eh! Eh!" that he wanted to go over there. I carried him over to David and the teacher. As I asked what had happened and why David was crying (he had woken from a bad dream screaming and crying), my son started patting him on the back and making cooing and "Ah, ah" sounds.

I needed to get to work, so after letting my son comfort David for a little while, I started walking away with my son still in my arms. I was going to take him to the room where the children would be playing who had napped already (he had napped at home with me). As I walked away, he protested loudly, "Eh! Eh!" and pointed back to David and his teacher. He wanted to go back.

When I brought him back, he comforted David some more. I soothingly said to my son, "Honey, we have to leave David and your teacher now. She's going to comfort him. He just woke up from a scary dream. He'll be okay. That was really nice and so sweet how comforting you were. Unfortunately I have to go to work now, so I need to bring you into the other room, otherwise I'd stay with you and David. I think your teacher will take good care of David. We should go in the other room."

He listened as I talked and seemed to understand. How did I know he understood? He didn't protest anymore or point to David; he just hugged me as I carried him to the play room.

After dropping him off, as I drove to my office I was amazed at his compassion and interest in David. I didn't know toddlers could be so involved in someone else's emotions, or want to be so sweet and caring. I realized it was a scene I'd never forget. I just loved that he was so compassionate and caring. I hope he gets to keep it as he grows up.

I remember one mother tearfully telling me about a visit to her in-laws. Upon their arrival, her toddler had immediately began to play with several objects within his reach. He was being gentle, but his grandfather said "No" to him. He looked confused and picked up one of the objects again. This time his grandpa said "No" more angrily and slapped his hand. The mother picked up her son to comfort him. Her father-in-law said, "You're going to spoil him rotten. He needs to learn the meaning of the word "No." The mother said, "Yes, he does, but at our house everything he can reach is a "Yes." We try to reserve "No" for dangerous things so it isn't a constant admonishment. Her father-in-law replied, "That's ridiculous!" The mom said, at this point, she was ready to leave but knew she was stuck there for the weekend.

She and her husband talked that night and decided they would try to explain some of the differences between old-style parenting and respectful parenting to his parents in the morning. If they seemed responsive, they would be asked to "play along" and see how well respectful parenting works. If they were not responsive, the young parents would try and do what they thought was right quietly with their son.

The next morning, just as the grandfather was about to admonish their child, the father took his son into his arms and said, "Grandpa and Grandma do things differently here than at home. That is something Grandpa says is not for playing. It is not a toy for you. Let's put it up here where it won't catch your eye as much." The grandfather looked on disapprovingly. At breakfast they broached the subject, found the grandparents disinterested, and dropped further attempts.

By Monday, the mom was frazzled by repeated examples of old-style parenting and entered my office, grateful to see someone who agreed with her and who would respond empathetically to the punitive nature of her weekend's encounters.

Good-Bye Terrible Twos, Hello Terrific Twos

Why not banish the concept of "the terrible twos" and replace it with "the terrific twos"? We know from educational research that labels are powerful. What you are called is what you become. A child labeled "slow" in school may actually be quite bright but may have trouble reaching her potential with a negative label. If a child's learning problems stem from problems at home and that child is having trouble concentrating because she's preoccupied with her home situation, a negative label could further hamper her intellectual progress and her self-esteem. Borrowing this idea from educational and developmental research, doesn't it make sense that if you perceive and verbally label your child's behavior as "oppositional," "acting out," rebellious," or "annoying," you'll be encouraging the kind of behavior you're labeling? Yet, that's exactly the behavior you want your child to be decreasing or eliminating.

Remember the words "You're a naughty child!" Guess what? Those words often resulted in you acting in a naughty way. Perhaps from stubborn pride, you decided at some level that you'd be good at something. At least you'd do naughty well. Or, maybe you wouldn't disappoint them because "naughty" is what they expected. You might have believed you were "naughty" rather than naughty being a description of your behavior.

Strategies

- **Listen with the idea that you're willing to change or compromise your ideas if your child suggests something you hadn't considered.**

- **If you don't like how you're viewing your child's behavior, refocus your view.** By refocusing your view, you're looking for another, more positive angle to view the current situation.

- **Focus on your child's curiosity, natural interest in learning, and desire to please.** Then talk to your child, providing information and choices so they can more easily behave in a way that is pleasing to them and to you.

- **Watch your child's frustration level and help your child set his own limits.**

Understanding Temper Tantrums

Oh, those "terrible twos," characterized by temper tantrums, whiny days, and struggling through what ought to be simple tasks like dressing or bathing. In truth, haven't you had moments as an adult when you wished you could cry, scream, and throw a few things? Especially when you're trying to learn something new and it isn't happening as easily as you would like? or what about when something emotional happens in your life? You want to be handling it differently, but you can't seem to deal with it as smoothly as you'd like? During those times, do you feel your emotions rumbling around inside? You might even want to let out a frustrated roar, but you're probably too "mature" or it's not the "appropriate" time or place. So you don't. You end up putting aside your feelings until there is a safe time and place to express them. Sometimes your feelings get lost while you're waiting for that safe place.

Are you ever secretly envious of your 2-year-old's ability to let it all out and not seem to care about the consequences? But then, of course, when they do let it all out, you probably have to shift back into the parent role. How you were parented will play a large role in how you deal with your 2-year-old's behavior. "Stop that nonsense!" was a common refrain in old-style parenting. If you think about it, what is nonsensical about letting out your feelings, be they frustration, anger, or exhaustion—especially if you're at your limit, and you don't know how to keep a lid on things yet?

Don't adults spend a lot of time, energy, therapy dollars, work-out time, or time sitting in seminars trying to learn how to "get in touch" with their emotions and express themselves more freely? Maybe some lessons from a 2-year-old would help. They have the "let-it-out system" down pat. They haven't been socialized into an emotionally constricted stance.

Let's look at it yet another way. What psychologists call "cognitive dissonance" is when a person can't make sense of two (or more) intellectual ideas and the person feels confused because she can't resolve the conflicting notions. "Emotional dissonance" is when a person feels all jumbled up inside and can't express herself in a rational manner. A 2-year-old caught up in the throes of emotions and having a classic temper tantrum is probably in the middle of experiencing emotional and/or cognitive dissonance. Her insides feel horrible and completely out of control, perhaps from her head all the way down to her toes.

How can adults relate to what your 2-year-old may be feeling when she is out of control? Have you ever been in the process of looking for a house? You find yourself involuntarily waking up in the middle of the night with a series of unending questions in your head: "Which house should I choose?" "Which would be the best investment?" "What if I get a lemon?" "Do I want to go for potential?" You want the questions to stop, but they won't. Night after night you wake up, the committees going at it in your head. You want to sleep but you can't. After a few days of stressful nights where you can't control your own thought patterns, do you know how raw you feel inside? That's when small things set you off. You're barely holding on to some degree of calmness.

Do you know how crazy looking for and purchasing a house can be? Yet, as an adult you have the emotional and intellectual wherewithal to cope with complicated situations. Try to remember those kinds of jumbled feelings when you are dealing with your 2-year-old, who only has a 2-year life experience pool to dip into. This example is a reasonable facsimile to what your 2-year-old feels inside when he is having a temper tantrum or stubbornly struggling over something that feels simple to you. It's not simple to him.

Frustration also often leads to temper tantrums in children. In adults it often leads to yelling, withdrawing, giving up, drinking, headaches, resentment, nervous stomach, high blood pressure, heart attacks, and ulcers. Can you imagine adults having temper tantrums in a New York subway car because it was too crowded, too hot, and they were going to be late for an appointment? I don't advocate encouraging your 2-year-old to have temper tantrums or having temper tantrums yourself. But when your child does "lose her composure," stand back a minute, and think, "Do I want to teach my child to suppress these feelings, or do I want to sympathize, listen, and teach her to express them differently?" Always begin by listening closely enough to be able to validate her feelings before asking her about other ways she could be expressing herself and then providing her with different options. You can do this with direct suggestions or leading her to options through a series of questions.

Dealing with Temper Tantrums

Let's say your child is in such emotional pain that he's yelling, kicking his feet, and flailing his arms. What if your heart went out to your child who was in such emotional pain and you thought something like, "He must be feeling so bad inside his body and mind right now. He deserves my love, not my admonishments to calm down." Thinking that way will lead you into a different way of behaving than how you might have been treated as a child.

If your child could be dealing with whatever is happening calmly, don't you think he would? What if you hugged him instead of being angry at him? What if he refuses your hugs, indicating he needs a bit of distance? How about some soothing talk: "I understand you're upset and it looks like you don't want me close right now. I'm going to leave you for a minute. When you have the words, let me know why you're upset, or show me how I can help."

What happens when you role model anger, disgust, irritation, and annoyance with 2-year-olds? They tantrum more because they are being taught the verbal part of temper tantrums. They're substituting flailing arms, kicking feet, and throwing themselves or objects around the room for verbally expressing annoyance or anger since they don't have sophisticated language skills. They can't express all their feelings verbally, so they use their bodies to help express their pent-up and overflowing feelings.

Instead of role modeling the kinds of behaviors you don't want to see, try to respect your child's emotional pain, which is as real as if he had been hit by a car and were in the hospital with injuries. You'd stand by him there. You'd sit at his bedside until he came to if he were unconscious. He needs you when he's emotionally upset and in emotional pain as much as he does when he's in physical pain. Remember, you may receive the brunt of the barrage, but he isn't doing it to you. He's just doing it, period.

In fact, if you are the object of his "attack" or "acting out," it's probably because he trusts you enough to be able to handle what feels like too much for him to keep inside. You'll know what to do. He wouldn't be putting it out there if he didn't need your responses to him on some level. His body, his mind, and his guts are doing it to him, and he's just expressing the extra stuff that's overflowing as best he can.

When you grow up in a family where there are two choices, either you're right or you're wrong, you never learn there are actually many different options in most situations. If you've internalized a two-option system, you're going to have a lot of trouble with your children as they're turning 2 because they're experiencing the world as a wonderfully blossoming place with so much to see, try out, and learn! Two choices, black and white, just won't work. You'll be blocking out the amorphous gray

Avoiding Temper Tantrums

- Anticipate building tension.
- Introduce something else to distract from the tension builder.
- Sympathize.
- Provide the words that describe the situation.
- Help your child with his or her struggle.
- Tell your child that it's okay to stop.
- Offer alternatives like a time-out to calm down or a less stressful alternative behavior.
- Lead them to other options through your questions.
- Give your child hugs and cuddles if they want closeness.

areas where all the fun and subtle learning is hiding. You'll probably be feeling like you're hitting your head against a brick wall if you try to impose such a constrained system on your 2-year-old. His world is opening up to him at such an incredible pace. His mind shouldn't be constrained by such a finite, confining system as bad or good, right or wrong, this way or that way. You'll feel a lot better the more flexible you can be.

Being flexible involves including your child as a full-fledged partner in a lot of decisions, negotiations, and options affecting your child's life, rather than dictating and dishing out judgments and edicts. I've included quite a few heartwarming stories in this chapter. When people use a respectful parenting approach with their children, they experience few full-blown, embarrassing, in-public, down on the floor, kicking and screaming temper tantrums. Their children don't need to, because they don't get to that level of frustration. Their parents see what's happening and intervene in a loving way before their child's emotional dissonance has mounted to an overwhelming level.

Linda: You know how some kids are taught to be artificially polite . . . like "Yes sir," "Yes ma'am," "Please," and "Thank you" for everything? I spent a few years in the South when I was growing up and I always hated that. That's why I was so surprised when I started hearing my 2-year-old daughter say "thank you" to things. I hadn't ever sat her down and taught her to say "thank you." But I guess my husband and I both would say "thank you" when she'd bring us things or give us things. She just picked up those words and their correct context and started using them, as if they were just part of her everyday language.

Cindy: My husband and I have always told our daughter stories. It seems to be a good way to get her to "get" stuff. Direct input doesn't work well with her, but metaphors in  story form that go right into her unconscious seem to work really well. Here's one my husband told her one evening . . . There was a Momma bear, a Papa bear, and a little girl bear named . . . (our daughter filled in the blank with Barbara). One day Barbara was playing with something dangerous and Papa Bear took it away from her. Barbara was mad. She said mean things, and cried. Papa Bear said, "This is our job. If we let you play with this, you could get hurt. Our job is to keep you safe. Your job is to play, but our job is to help you play with things that will be fun and where you can't get hurt."

After a story like that, it would be easier for a while. We could remind her about the bears, and she had an easier time cooperating with our limits.

I've also learned how helpful songs can be. Sometimes my daughter can hear things in a song that she would have trouble hearing more directly. So I make up lots of songs. Like for weaning. I had thought I would wait until she was ready to wean, but when my daughter was about 2½, I was ready and didn't want to wait for her to be ready. I also didn't want to upset her, since nursing had always been too nice to spoil it with an abrupt halt. I wanted to introduce the idea of weaning in a gentle way, getting her to be part of this process.

I started singing a song about a little girl named (her name) who liked to nurse a lot. For a few days I sang her the verse about how much she liked to nurse. Then I added a verse about other things she liked to do. A few days later I added a verse about how big she was getting, and how many things she could do now that she couldn't do before. Finally, I added a verse saying she was so big, she didn't even want to nurse anymore. She liked the song and at times that we would have nursed in the past, I sang her the song, especially the verse about how big she was, that she didn't want to nurse anymore. It worked! We weaned pretty easily using the song and lots of cuddles.

I worked with a woman who came in saying her 2-year-old was driving her crazy. I asked her if she could be more specific. She said, "Whenever we go someplace and Jason is enjoying himself, he throws a fit when it's time to leave and I'm embarrassed. I mean, it's to the point where I don't want to go anywhere." I asked this women if she ever gave her son a warning before trying to get him to leave, or if she ever sympathized with him about how difficult it is to stop having fun and shift gears. She said she hadn't tried any of that. We talked some more and she was ready to try it.

The next week she came in and said, "I was at my friend's house and our children were playing so nicely. I figured it would be hard when it was time to go, but I tried what we talked about. First I went over and said, 'Jason, I'm so glad you're having so much fun. You're playing really nicely with Scott. I want you to know we'll be leaving soon and I'll give you one more warning before we go.' He looked up at me and kept playing.

"Then a little while later, when I went over for the second warning, I said, 'Jason, this is the second warning I told you about. Now we're going to help you two clean up and then we'll be going home. I hope you can cooperate so we can come back again soon. It's clean-up time now. Let's see how quickly we can all clean up. Should we sing a song as we clean up?' He was distracted by the song and he left happily in my arms as we waved to our friends."

> **Cindy:** You know what they say about 2-year-olds and temper tantrums? Well, my daughter hasn't had those. I mean, maybe a few times she's laid on the floor and cried, but she

hasn't had any of those lie-down, scream, kick your feet, flail your arms out of control ones I'd been warned about. You know, the reason most people refer to a child's second year as "the Terrible Twos." She's 2 ½ now, and with me being pregnant and all, I just don't think we're going to get those.

Maybe if children are listened to, respected, validated, and helped through difficult times, they won't have the kinds of frustrations that lead to temper tantrums. If tensions are eased with understanding hugs and soothing words, maybe the children won't need to tantrum.

If You Had a Traumatic Childhood

To respect children, to validate them, to be there for them, you'll need to disconnect from your old tapes. You'll need to move a few giant steps away from your personal history if you were "scolded" when you were "bad." You were probably never "bad" in the sense of being an ax murderer. Perhaps you broke something by accident and got blamed as if you did it on purpose. Perhaps you broke something on purpose because you weren't getting any kind of response from your parent and you had to do something to get them to notice you. But were you *bad?* No, in that case you were creative to think of something you could do to get their attention, which you so desperately needed but weren't getting.

When I work with people, I often point out that what they did when they were small children was necessary to cope in an unhealthy situation. I congratulate them for finding a way to cope, even if it didn't bring them the kind of loving attention they really wanted. They couldn't have survived in their family of origin without some of what they did. Yet, their attempts to cope often backfired because they didn't get the love and respectful, gentle attention they intuitively knew they needed. Instead, they often got yelled at, spanked, or worse. But at least they tried to get something. They tried, in their own creative way, to break through the emotional vacuum their parents presented.

It can be empowering for adults to see their childhood efforts, which they had viewed for years as ineffective or futile, as necessary creative coping strategies that they came up with on their own and that indeed helped them survive in their dysfunctional homes.

Here's an example of old-style parenting and one 2-year-old's attempt to break through his mother's neglect. A young woman had just left her husband. She had a 2-year-old little boy. The poor boy was dragged around and often neglected by his mother, who was preoccupied with a few new men in her life. One day she came home and left her son asleep in the car outside (he was napping). He woke up screaming, clearly frightened or disoriented to find himself in the car alone. She brought him inside and proceeded to ignore him again while she talked for a long time on the phone with a new boyfriend. As she talked on the phone, she had placed her child at the table where she was serving him dinner while still largely ignoring him . . .

The little boy tried to get her attention. First saying, "Mommy, Mommy" over and over again, in a normal tone of voice. She responded by cupping her hand over the phone and telling him to wait. After a few minutes he tried yelling, "Mommy, Mommy." She again cupped her hand over the phone saying with exasperation, "I'm on the phone! You have to have some patience!" Patience? Who was kidding who? This kid had been left in the car, allowed to wail until she deemed it time to go get him from the car, then plunked down at the kitchen table to be told to wait some more.

His next response? He pulled down his shorts and proceeded to pee all over the table. Horrified by his behavior, she put the phone down long enough to yell at him, asking him what the hell he was doing, and grabbed him from the table, telling him he wasn't getting any dinner that night. She was punishing him for his 2-year-old behavior, rather than looking at *her* own neglectful adult behavior that caused *his* behavior.

Peeing all over the hastily prepared dinner was a great way to get this woman's attention. Was this child bad? No. The mother was being neglectful at best. She had withdrawn from him. She was not doing her job physically or emotionally. Her attention was captivated by her boyfriends, and this little boy was saying, "ENOUGH! NOTICE ME!" loud and clear, although he didn't have the words to express it directly.

Maybe he had needed to pee all the time he had been saying "Mommy," and when she didn't help him down from the chair so he could go potty, he had just done the best he could. We'll never know. But for whatever reason, he had resorted to peeing all over the table.

Unfortunately, he didn't get any loving attention after his action. He got her wrath and the punishment of being sent (alone) to his room. How sad. Old-style parenting versus respectful parenting.

You don't have to set your child up for needing to break through a vacuum of emotional distance. You can be close right from the start. You can respect this little human being's basic right to be loved, understood, held, and coddled. Your children also have the right to be left alone when necessary—but do make frequent trips back to see if they're ready for the cuddles and loving they're wanting but not yet able to accept.

Power Struggles

Strategies

- Sympathize with your child's feelings.
- Ask your child if there is a different way he'd rather be behaving.
- Ask for his ideas and offer your own.
- Calm down together.
- Try the new option.

Through careful attentive interactions, parents are able to guide their children through potentially frustrating experiences. When children do "start losing it," respectful parents don't lay additional "trips" on their children by being angry, annoyed, or judgmental about their behavior. Instead they feel and express sympathy for their child's emotional discomfort and the children feel understood by their parents' attention, which in turn helps ease their discomfort.

This is not to say that children never have temper tantrums or power struggles. But often parents can diffuse a power struggle by asking themselves, "How important is this right now?" "What will really happen if he gets his shoes on in five, ten, or two minutes?" "Do I need to insist and go at it head on when she's not quite ready, or can I role model flexibility by saying, 'It looks like you're not ready to put your shoes on right now.' I think that'll be okay. I can go for the flexibility. "Why don't you play with that truck a little longer and then we can try getting your shoes on again? How about if I come back in two minutes?'"

The child gets to play a little more. He also gets a sense of being able to manipulate his way in this world (in a positive sense). The parent is teaching the child about negotiating, patience, flexibility, and understanding. Nine times out of ten, two minutes later the child is willing to cooperate.

Power struggles can often be sidetracked or avoided with a little creative thinking and questioning by parents. Some parents do this in their head, while other parents find it helpful when they hear themselves ask out loud, "Is this really so important that we have to struggle about it?" Somehow, hearing the words often helps them realize that it isn't so important, and they can figure out another way of handling the situation. In old-style parenting, if parents "gave in" it was considered capitulating, losing ground, spoiling your child, losing respect for you as *the* authority in the household. What hogwash. In respectful parenting, there is no such notion as old-time "giving in." Instead, flexibility is seen as a means to an end: both you and your child's needs and wants can be met in the most peaceful and loving way possible.

Who says you're the only one who should be respected (as in old-style parenting)? How about giving your child dignity and respect? Giving children dignity and respect leads to less acting-out behavior. They don't have to resort to "inappropriate behaviors." You're circumventing the problem, heading it off at the pass, avoiding the need to act out by providing loving guidance or assistance to your child at the first indication that it's needed.

After working through your old parenting issues and incorporating respectful parenting ideas into your daily life with your 2-year-old, the next task is to support and encourage your child's independence and not push him too hard when he's not *really* ready—even though he may look and act ready at first. If he starts crying after trying new things (like running farther away from you than he ever did before), he may be telling you, "I thought I could do it, but now that I'm trying, I'm not so sure I'm so ready. Hold me a while, so I know you're still there and I'm still safe."

Defusing Power Struggles

- Be aware of building tension and back off.
- Give yourself a time-out and ask yourself if this is really important.
- Give your child a time-out.
- Tell yourself and your child, "I don't like what's happening here. Let's both put our heads together and come up with a different way of handling the situation."
- Say, "I want to do this peacefully, do you?"
- Give your child other options.
- Have a good laugh at the whole situation.

Amy: One day, when my son was about one month shy of being 3 years old, I arrived at day care to pick him up and found a little plastic baggy in his cubby with a little rock inside and a note, "Dan's rock." I thought, "Oh, how cute. He found a special treasure rock and the teachers set it aside for him." When I went to thank the teachers for their extra effort and inquire about the story behind the rock, I got a different picture. Apparently, my son had stuck this little rock up his nose. He had been brought to the office, and luckily another mother, who was a nurse, was able to get it out with a tweezers. I was more than a little surprised.

As my child and I were walking toward our car, I talked to him about the seriousness of putting things in his nose and told him how dangerous it was, and that I didn't want him to do it again. As I finished, I looked at him, expecting his usual response of "Okay Mommy." Instead, he looked at me and said, "Well, I will if I want to." I was about to crack up but I knew this was serious. So I repeated my explanation adding to the end, "And if you do that again I'll just have to ask your teacher to give you a time-out." His eyes opened wider as he said, "Okay, Mommy." He hates time-outs, and the threat of one was enough to get his attention.

After he was in his car seat, I was thinking, as I drove away, that this was the first evidence of a changing child. He had always been a compliant, reasonable, easy child. Here he was growing up. I wasn't sure I was up for this one. It had been hard not to laugh, but I sensed that this first act of defiance had to be dealt with "right," or at least seriously. But it was pretty funny. Of all things for him to get independent about, the "right" to stick a rock up his nose?

Pacifiers

I think some of the biggest power struggles ensue when parents decide it is time to not use the pacifier anymore. Remember, that is a parental decision and if you make it categorically without consulting your young child, unless you happen to arrive at that decision at the same time as your child, you may be in for some trouble. Pacifiers are one of those primitive pleasures in early life. You allow your infant and baby to have them so she feels secure, so she feels comfortable, so she can soothe herself. Since you've given her that privilege, don't just snatch it away. Be gradual and use those sophisticated techniques of distraction and communication. Talk to her about how big she is getting and how she may not need it anymore. Ask your child if she's ready to try not having the pacifier for a few minutes. You could even set a kitchen timer for periods of time. Ensure success by having some sense of how long she can go without it when she's engaged in another activity, and begin the timer with a time you know she can handle already. Gradually ask her if she wants to see how long she can go. Reinforce her progress rather than rushing her too quickly.

Pacifiers are a very personal thing. You might ask her if she'd like a special stuffed animal now that she doesn't need her pacifier at night anymore. Take it slowly and if there are a few "slips" to wanting it again, make sure you respond kindly and respectfully to that, too. One step forward and half a step back is still progress. Remember that you'll get there—your child will not be entering kindergarten with a pacifier in her mouth. So don't get anxious if your child doesn't meet your initial suggestions enthusiastically. It's another one of those times where you want to suggest and lead but not force, then follow your child's natural pace once she knows where you're heading. Work with your child and make it a mutual effort. You want your child to know that you want to help her so it's a comfortable, good experience for both of you.

If your child is really adamant about not giving up her pacifier and you've tried everything in this book, consider what else is going on in your child's life. Think about what other changes are happening and why she might be needing it. See if there is anything you can do to make her world a safer place so she can feel comfortable and soothed in other ways. If necessary, you could consult with a professional who can help you assess the situation and see why your child is needing that extra soothing she gets from her pacifier and can help you make her world a little safer so you can again pursue retiring the pacifier. Or, when in doubt, wait and try again a few weeks or months later. If this is done on a mutually agreed upon time frame, it should be a relatively easy process.

I've certainly encountered a number of families where the pacifier has "mysteriously disappeared" and the child is told that "it was lost" or "I can't find it," and requests for purchasing another are met with evasions. Children do survive that transition. I still prefer the more thoughtful and mutually agreed upon transition where everyone is honest and above board. I think it is an important precedent to set—I'll be honest and respectful with you and I'd like the same in return. In my book, it's not a good excuse to "lie for convenience." If you can lie for convenience, watch as your children learn to lie for convenience to keep themselves out of trouble.

Potty Training

A common source of developmental frustration for parents and children is potty training. Especially when parents try to potty *train*, instead of having it happen more naturally. In this situation, the child's frustration often stems from the parents' impatience and frustration. Parents are ready for no more diapers and so they introduce the potty seat. If the child is not as ready, the child won't be able to do what the parents want. It's a developmental impossibility.

When that reality isn't accepted, parents become disappointed, frustrated, angry, even disgusted at the prospect of endless diapers. If parents express or ooze these feelings and their young child feels their frustration, the child will be upset also. An upset young child certainly will not be able to perform successfully in the potty department.

What a great setup for a vicious cycle of a child holding her poop and pee because she's picking up on her parents' tension. The parents, in turn, get more tense because the child is not accomplishing what they want the child to accomplish, namely using the potty. It's a great example of how parents' and children's tensions feed on each other. Potty "training" is often a stress-filled, frustrating situation that ultimately, at some point in time, results in success. But like most frustrating situations, there are easier ways to the goal, if you take the time to explore other angles.

Throwing out the expression "potty training" may be a helpful first move. Why think about "training" a toddler or 2-year-old? She's not ready for regimented training of any kind. She learns better by experimentation, modeling, and sensing. If you can leave her naked in the summer around the time you think she may be ready, she'll be able to feel her own body sensations better than being encased in a big diaper. If a little potty seat is left in the bathroom next to or near Mommy and Daddy's potty, then she may get the idea on her own and go running for her potty when it's time.

"Accidents" are bound to happen. They can be dealt with lovingly and in a nonjudgmental manner. Not getting to the potty in time or forgetting about the potty entirely is part of the process of learning how your body works. *If* no big deal is made and *if* the child is developmentally ready, then it'll happen fairly easily. On the other hand, if you want her to use the potty, and she's not ready to give up the security and ease of her diapers, she'll let you know by having frequent "accidents." You have a choice to make. Either you continue and frustrate yourself and her, or you decide to calmly say, "I seem to have made a mistake. It's not time for the little potty yet. That's okay. We'll try it again in a while, and maybe then you'll want to use it."

If you say you made a mistake, you won't feel like your child failed and your child won't feel like she failed you. Putting off using the potty does not become a blow to her self-esteem. In addition, you have modeled being human, making mistakes, taking responsibility for your mistakes by admitting them, and changing your course of action. By doing so, you all learn valuable lessons.

The examples from this chapter and others will go a long way toward helping you experience the wonders of the Terrific Twos with your child. Enjoy!

Discipline for You and Your Child

Old Style Discipline

Occasionally I've run into remarkably rigid, so-called well-behaved children who sit with their hands folded on their laps and look rather blindly in front of them, waiting for their parent's permission to pick up a fork and eat. They don't look happy. If you look closely, there's usually a hyper-vigilant look in their eye, as if they've been frightened into obedience. If childhood is not about fun, creativity, and exploring your world's boundaries, then later you will set up your life to be more of the same—restrictive. You run into several risks when you use restrictive, rigid parenting methods. Children will often swing to an opposite extreme and rebel because they haven't been introduced to the gray area in between rigid control and acting out. They may choose a mate who will control them. Or they may join a cult where a leader will tell them what to do.

How were you disciplined? Were you spanked, hit, beaten, yelled at, berated, threatened, given time-outs, sent to your room, given the silent treatment, or sent off to relatives? Did your parent "go away" by withholding affection or attention? Did they take away your favorite toys? Or did they take the time and talk to you about what was happening, what they wanted to be happening, and how to handle the discrepancy?

Some families talked after they had yelled, hit, or spanked. These families needed to let out their tensions first, and then they could attempt to talk. Sometimes issues were resolved and they were able to avoid the same situation again; other times it became a revolving-door pattern of anger, hitting, screaming, and talking again. Sometimes family members gave up hope that things would ever change; sometimes each new bout of anger brought fresh disappointment. Respectful parenting offers many other options and considers any alternatives used on previous generations of small children to be unnecessary and sometimes unacceptable.

Respectful Discipline

Strategies

- **Give your child positive messages.** Rather than saying, "Don't spill your milk," or "Be careful not to spill your milk," say, "You're doing a nice job of holding your sippy cup," or "I like how carefully you're drinking your milk." Wording messages positively helps assure the response you want.

- **Look for the positive intent in your child's behavior or a more positive interpretation you can put on it.** Ask yourself, "What could my child possibly be telling me?" You can also look at what is occurring within a broader context, thereby seeing a more complete picture. By looking at the context in which the behavior is occurring, you'll see things you're blocking out. This additional information will probably enable you to be more understanding with your child.

- **If you don't like how you're viewing your child's behavior, refocus your view. By refocusing your**

view, you're looking for another, more positive angle to view the current situation. When you see the current situation in a more positive light, you will feel differently about it and you can respond to it in a more caring way. It's like putting a new lens on your camera and seeing a more complete picture with a wider angle than you were seeing with a finely focused lens.

- **When you're in a power struggle with your child, back off for at least 30 seconds.** By backing off, you'll clear your mind a little. Remind yourself that you're the adult here and you need to give the situation another look, rather than being caught in a power struggle with an 18-month-old. There's always a different way to handle the situation than head on. Backing off gives you the breathing room to figure out a more creative solution to the dilemma at hand.

- **Set reasonable limits and be willing to repeat them as your child's curiosity tests those limits.** Limits with small children need to be repeated over and over because children honestly and easily forget when they are at play and having fun.

- **Pick the important stuff to make your points.** Don't struggle and teach all day long.

- **Make sure that your limits are appropriate and reasonable.**

Small children do need limits or consequences for their behavior, but the old methods won't build healthy self-esteem in your children. Young children need encouragement to express themselves. They need safe boundaries so they don't hurt themselves. Safety can be established without telling them they are *bad* for touching something that has come within their reach. They are not *bad;* they are simply exploring, using their curiosity and intelligence. Perhaps their explorations are challenging to you, as a parent, to keep them (and your valuables) safe, but that's part of your responsibility in being a parent. If you aren't doing your job well, they shouldn't be punished for it.

Refocusing Your View

When your child tells you he's had enough (in his own way), rather than seeing a small child's actions as malicious or aimed against you, you could see your small child communicating as best he can (even if it's a temper tantrum or a crying fit in the middle of your shopping trip). Other times, if he touches too many things or wants to wander off, you can see him as a naturally curious human being.

Example: One woman I was working with came in around Christmas time, obviously frustrated. When I asked her what was upsetting her, she told me about her 11-month-old daughter who kept crawling over to the Christmas tree and pulling on the branches and ornaments. The child had unwittingly shaken off her favorite one, which broke when it hit the floor. The mother was frustrated because she had told her daughter repeatedly not to touch, yet the small girl insisted on crawling over to the "No-No tree." In addition, the mother was upset that her favorite ornament had been broken. After talking for a while she admitted that she was angry because her baby wasn't listening to her. Her anger was heightened because, as a result of her baby not listening, her favorite ornament was broken. All her emotions were understandable from the mother's perspective, and I empathized with her.

But after some empathy, I said, "I think you've lost perspective on the whole picture. Let's look at your daughter's side now. Can you imagine yourself as your daughter? Okay, you're crawling along, minding your own business, checking out the living room, where you know you have a lot of toys, and during your regular routine you come across a new, large, glittering, beautiful object. Well, it appears to be a tree. Indeed, upon closer inspection you find it is a tree. But this tree is different—it's inside the house (in your domain) and it has pretty things you can just about grab onto if you reach and reach. And you do. But OOPS, here comes Mommy and she doesn't look happy."

"Why is she looking at you like that? Her voice sounds sharp and she's saying 'No! No!' Then she's picking you up and carrying you away from that beautiful tree. Usually she encourages you to explore new things and points out pretty things to look at or gives you nice things to touch. But here she's taking you away and saying 'No! No!' Why? When it's so big and so beautiful and so obviously there for the...what? Just to sit? Couldn't be...and back you crawl again. Your curiosity is captured. You're enthralled: it's so big! You look at its texture, the decorations, their colors, shapes, sheen. They dance when you touch the tree. How could you, as an excited baby, be expected to leave it alone? OOPS! One broke. You didn't maliciously decide to break Mommy's favorite ornament. You don't even have the concepts of malicious, or favorite, or even that what you touch may hurt you (the tree fall?) or hurt something else (the ornament?).

Once the mother saw that perspective, her tension visibly disappeared and she started laughing, "I set my daughter up, didn't I? I expected too much from her. Of course she couldn't listen to me. I see it now. But what do we do now? I still want to have Christmas."

Together, we worked out some compromises. The Christmas tree was put inside the portable crib so her daughter could see it but not touch it. A fall-back plan was that for this year, it could be put on the deck so she could see it through the glass doors, but not be able to touch it. We also decided the mother should take down any other ornaments she wouldn't want to see broken and not use them for a couple of years.

Although she had been about to put some presents under the tree to make the living room look even more festive, she decided not to put any presents out until after her daughter was asleep on Christmas Eve. We also talked about how she could talk to her child about how exciting and enchanting all the colors were, and how special having a tree inside was. I encouraged the mother to tell her daughter about early memories she had about Christmas and to share her daughter's fascination and excitement instead of squelching it.

Plan Ahead

A different way of dealing with potentially unacceptable behavior is to plan around it so you can avoid difficult situations. When parents anticipate their child's abilities to deal with an event, they can make plans that will fit their child's abilities rather than pushing their child into handling more than she can—which usually results in an overtired, overstimulated, or overanxious child.

Put It Away

Another basic preventive idea is to remember that anything within your child's reach or climbing sphere is fair play. If she can get it, she can play with it. You could consider it part of your job as a parent to modify your house and its contents. As your baby toddles, and as his world gets larger because of his climbing abilities, there's more to move. Many parents find it easier to put mementos or breakable objects away for a couple of years. Then the baby is free to completely let his imagination and curiosity be his guide in exploring his world. You are free to enjoy his explorations rather than fearing for a memento's safety or wondering how to refocus your anger as he reaches for yet another breakable object. If those objects aren't around, that part of limit setting is not necessary. See how "limit setting" can be used rather than old-fashioned discipline?

Give Them More Time or Space

An alternative method that works well with children is to stand back from the situation and give them a little time or space. For instance, if you're trying to get your child ready for day care and she wants to play, you can either get into a power struggle or you can say, "I can see you want to play now, and I was hoping we could get you dressed. I'm going to go now and when you're ready to get dressed, let me know." Standing right outside her door is usually far enough to give her the space she needs to decide to cooperate and allows you a safe distance to monitor her. Invariably, within 30 seconds, having handed the "control" over to your child, she will come back and say "I'm ready" or present herself to you dressed as best as she can do.

Children are struggling for mastery and control over their environment. Providing them with opportunities within your needs helps both of you get what you want: the task done and a sense of accomplishment. A simple but sincere "thank you" when your child does come around can make the next time easier. Your child will remember how nice it felt to be appreciated and acknowledged for being cooperative.

Example: When your child pulls all your plastic containers out of a cabinet, strews them across the kitchen making a huge mess, and looks up at you with delight written across his face, rather than being upset and seeing his behavior as mischievous, enjoy his sense of mastery at this marvelously detailed feat he has just accomplished. Tell him he sure did a thorough job. Laugh with him, and then show him how much fun it can be trying to get the containers back in the cabinet. See if he can hand you one and then commend him for his help. Have fun with him.

Give Them Choices

Another idea is to say, "We need to brush your teeth and get dressed now. Which would you like to do first?"

"Brush teeth first."

"Okay, let's do it in the order you suggested, we'll brush your teeth and then we'll get dressed." A nod of the head in agreement. In this example the child was able to talk, but these same ideas can be used with preverbal children. As long as they can point, they can express their desires. Just watch where their little finger points and you'll have the answers to your questions.

Whenever possible give a little by respecting your child's desire to have a say in what you do, or ask your child what she'd like to do first, or how she'd like to accomplish the tasks necessary to leave the house. It helps to repeat back to her what your understanding of the situation is to make sure you heard her correctly, or to make sure she knows what she said, and that she still wants to do things the way she blurted it out, because I've seen that change, too. It's human prerogative—we're fickle beings. Remember: children are also entitled to their fickle moments, and if you can allow for them to occasionally change their mind, they'll be more flexible when you change your mind.

Be Creative and Flexible

Being a healthy and loving parent is one of the most intellectually and creatively challenging tasks in life. You have to come up with new ideas, new ways of doing things as your child grows, questions, and tests your limits. Children don't wait for adolescence to test boundaries. They're rehearsing in their first few years for the next big time of challenging limits in adolescence. Be creative, not rigid. Follow through and be consistent so your child knows you mean what you say. Consistent and creative— what a combination.

When you consistently let your child know that no matter what she does, you'll love her; no matter what he does or says, he's lovable; she's unique and you're doing your best to help her blossom and flourish; he needs to be kept safe and you're there to help him be safe, then you create a safe, acceptable environment in which your child can explore and grow. Use your creativity to express these concepts to your children. When you're feeling challenged by his behavior, sometimes gentle holding and soothing talk helps. Sometimes, tell a child you care, but you've tried everything you can think of and now you're going to leave him be for a few minutes—but when he thinks you can help he should come and let you know.

Cindy: My 2½-year-old daughter has a strong will. Once she gets on something it's sometimes difficult to get her off it. One day, as I was cooking dinner, she started in with "I want to paint, I want to paint," so I took the time to get her paints out and went back to dinner. Almost immediately, she started saying, "I want water, I want water." I said, "I'm in the middle of cooking, please give me a minute and I'll get you the water." But that wasn't fast enough for her. She continued with, "I want water, I want water," louder and louder, switching to "WANT IT NOW! WANT NOW!" In the middle of that, just when I was going to get angry, I saw her father coming up the driveway and said cheerily, "Oh look, Daddy's outside, let's go see him." We went outside, she forgot about painting, I came back in and cooked dinner, and he took over with her. Sometimes diversion is necessary, especially when you have a few children and the task at hand needs to get done. I suppose if I hadn't forgotten the water for the paints, part of that episode could have been avoided. I did the best I could.

Time-Outs

When big and little people feel backed in a corner, or they're stuck in a power struggle, some breathing space almost always helps. I call that space a "time-out" or "cool-out time." A person can figure things out faster in a calmer setting without the stressors of the moment interfering. Then she can come to her own decision, plus she'll feel more in control of her decision after calming down and thinking about things more objectively. Telling your child to take a time-out or giving yourself a time-out is not punishment! It's simply a time to get a different perspective and come up with solutions that will allow you to get unstuck and continue the day peacefully. Grown-ups need time-outs at least as much as children because children are usually reacting to their parents' emotional energy. Time-outs are not meant to be long. Sometimes just saying, "I need a time-out" is enough to cool yourself down. Sometimes, 30 seconds to 3 minutes are needed. All it takes is enough time to change your mood and your behavior (including your tone of voice) to come back with an explanation of what happened and an effective plan to avoid whatever just happened to cause the need for a time-out.

Sylvia: My son, (he's 2½) seems to appreciate time-outs. Like the other day, he was having a temper tantrum for no reason that I could tell. Nothing was wrong...I said, "Maybe you need a time-out?" He went over to the couch, climbed up (that's his time-out place), and sat quietly for less than a minute. He came back over to me saying, "I'm okay now." It was all over. He just needed a way to get out of it himself, and the nonstimulation in time-out did the trick.

Another day, he was getting upset with a toy, and he said, "Mommy, think I need time-out," and over he went for a minute or so. When he came back he had a big smile on his face. I think he was feeling good because he had been able to get himself in a better mood.

When You Are Frustrated or Angry

Sometimes letting yourself cry helps. Sometimes, rather than imposing a rigid rule, try admitting you don't know how to handle something, saying you want to think about it, considering your options, coming back with a workable alternative, and explaining it. Sometimes what helps is calling a friend on the phone or a spouse from another room to take over. But the same thing does not work every time. Each situation, and each child within each situation, is different. To further complicate matters, the first three years are so chock full of change and development that what was useful a few weeks ago may not work right now, but it probably will work if you try it again at a later date. Rotating options and always being open to new suggestions helps you parent creatively and respectfully.

Dealing with Your Frustration

Here's an example. In a calm tone of voice, the parent describes in specific terms what happened: "I just went into your room to shut off the light and saw your trucks and stuffed animals on the floor. I thought we had agreed that you'd put them away."

The child just looks at you.

Then you tell your child your reactions or feelings, taking as much responsibility for your feelings as possible without blaming or judging. You could also ask for help in understanding what happened (so you don't jump to your own conclusions). "I was a little surprised to see them still there. I wonder what happened?"

"I don't know."

A small child often doesn't know. He's not saying that to get you angry, so you could suggest something nonthreatening and see what happens. "Well, since you had agreed before, could you pick them up now?"

"Okay," or maybe, "Will you help?"

You have the choice of helping or attending to something else. Helping will assure the task gets done and will reestablish the two of you as a team rather than adversaries.

Staying Organized

Whose home is orderly where there is at least one young child? Around the time you're returning to work from maternity leave, look around. When it's completely unclear where the hours in the day are to work, nurture, nurse, change diapers, shop for food, prepare meals, eat, wash dishes, do laundry, sleep, and clean, remember: *something has to give.* Choose at least one item on the list and figure out a way you don't have to do it yourself. (You may also need to lower your standards.)

Even if you need to have a sense of orderliness around you, if you're juggling work and family, or even just juggling a multiple-child family and no outside-the-home job, you need to "give" somewhere in your life. One strategy is to spontaneously change your plans and expectations as the day unfolds. Rather than sticking to prearranged ideas that no longer apply because of things like a child who won't take a nap, an earlier nap than planned, a grumpy parent or child, bad weather, or an unplanned tummy ache, simply change your plans. Flexibility and spontaneity will enable you to avoid countless unnecessary power struggles with your child.

Creating Consequences

Respectful parenting does advocate boundaries and consequences. Whenever possible, they ought to be prearranged so your child knows they're coming. One example is an adult's work schedule. If there's a time when a parent must be at work, then flexibility in the morning has a natural limit. One parent trying to work this out with her 2-year-old reported being completely stumped. She didn't know how to handle her daughter's refusal to get dressed. She had tried talking, cajoling, yelling, and threatening, but she was still always late for work, and her boss was beginning to give her a hard time.

We talked about it and she recognized that dressing had become a power struggle with her daughter and wondered if perhaps it was a way for her daughter to "have" her mother for a few extra minutes. We came up with the following plan. The next day she was going to talk to her daughter before dressing time arrived, so she had time to adjust to the next thing on her morning's agenda. At that time, the mother was also going to talk to her about how Mommy has to go to work, and it would be nice if she could cooperate so they could both start their days cheerfully instead of being sad and frustrated. She could point out to her daughter that she (the daughter) really had the power to make the choice of a fun morning or an unhappy one.

If talking did not do the trick, then the mother was not going to struggle or cajole. She was going to calmly tell her daughter the consequence of not cooperating and that if she didn't get dressed easily, the mother was going to carry through with her consequence by calmly picking out an outfit, taking her child to day care in her pajamas, and having her get dressed there when she was ready.

At our next session, the mother reported that the talk did not work the first day. But as she was putting her daughter in her car seat in her pajamas she started saying, "I'm ready. Get dressed now." The mom agreed to go back into the house and change her (she had left some extra time just in case), but warned her daughter that she would not do that again. The next day, when the mother again started talking to her about the upcoming getting-dressed time, her daughter said, "I pick out," and her mother said "Fine." Since then, they have had smooth mornings taking turns picking out her clothes.

When children are given choices, they have a sense of control, such as the little girl in the last example. Children will often choose to stay within reasonable boundaries and limits. They will also develop a sense of pride from being involved in decisions. Whereas, when children are expected or forced (through coercion and punishment) to meekly submit, their self-esteem is shot down each time.

Setting Limits

Limits are important in respectful parenting. Without limits, respectful parenting backfires because you give too much. You can give to the point where you are depleted, flat, impatient, and irritable, because you're stretched too thinly. Your child can become a "taker" instead of a taker and a giver. You will be unhappy with the results. Just the way you want to respect your child and not bombard his system with too much stimuli so he can't think straight or feel rational, you also need to do the same with yourself.

You have to respect your own limits and teach your child how to respect your limits so you have energy to spare, especially for those random sleepless nights that come along. Your brain needs to recognize its limits. It's okay to say to your toddler, "Daddy is so tired tonight, we need to just play quietly tonight and cuddle so Daddy can be patient with you." Sharing your limits teaches your child there are choices. When you're tired, you can push yourself to a point where you get stimulation overload; you're irritable and that's no fun for you or anyone around you. Or, you can recognize you've had enough, slow down, be peaceful, and it will be pleasant for you and everyone around you.

Respectul parenting is a two-way street. Mutual respect for yourself and others encourages gentleness and peace in your household. It also encourages flexible and logical thinking, listening to your feelings, and looking at a situation and all its parts before jumping to conclusions. It encourages everyone in your house to feel, listen, see, and think things through thoroughly. These are the greatest gifts you can give your children because they are life-long gifts they can use on a daily basis, and they don't cost a cent. Taking the time to do this kind of parenting guides you into setting reasonable limits that will replace traditional discipline.

Punishment

Certainly there are times when an age-appropriate consequence is in order. But again, the term punishment can be viewed differently than it was viewed in the past. Punishment was usually given out from the parents' anger level rather than in relation to the "indiscretion." Children are born innocent, pure, and good. They are not naturally malicious, bad, spiteful little beings. They may learn some of that along the way, but they have to see it or experience it to learn it.

When children are loved and respected, they will love and respect others. Certainly they will test the limits you lovingly set. They will not always follow through with something you negotiated with them, and you will get frustrated, disappointed, and angry at times. Just the way it's important for you to follow through on your commitments, children need to know it's important for them to be consistent and do what they said they would do. A lot of potentially volatile situations can be defused depending upon your attitude.

If you begin feeling angry and say to yourself (hopefully, not out loud), "Darn it, why didn't he put his toys away! We talked about it, and he agreed. Now we have to leave and all his trucks and stuffed animals are on the floor. Why didn't that (bad?) boy listen!?" From there you might yell, yank, and criticize your child for not behaving or listening. A struggle and unpleasant scene would follow. Or, you could take a one-minute time-out to calm yourself down.

Ask yourself why you're getting so angry. Are you doing what your parents did to you? Do you want to? If your answers to the last two questions are yes and no, and you want to handle this relatively minor infraction differently, then before approaching your child directly, figure out exactly what he did or did not do in behaviorally specific terms. No value judgments—just specifics. Try to refocus your child's behavior in the most positive light.

You might come up with this: your child said he would put the toys away and he didn't. That part is simple. But why didn't he? Was he testing your limits, and if so was he trying to get you mad? Was he trying to find out how his little world operates so he knows and can choose his own limits rather than submitting to yours? When you're calm, you'll realize your child probably didn't do this to "get to you." If he did, there was probably good reason. Maybe you were preoccupied and ignoring him for a long time. This might have been the only way he could get your attention. If it wasn't that, what was it?

Perhaps he forgot or got so caught up in playing as he handled the toys (intending to put them away) that somehow the cleaning task got lost. Or something else you haven't thought of. At that point, your curiosity could be piqued, you could tell your child how you were feeling, and ask him what happened. Together you could figure out how to deal with it.

A short time-out allows you to figure out behaviorally what has happened and how you *really* feel about it. Perhaps your flare of anger is your own personal history with your parents' reactions. Often, though, anger is a symptom of some other underlying emotion—like hurt, sadness, fear, surprise, disappointment, or even frustration at an approaching deadline and an unfinished task. You might recognize the need to allow more time for yourself, perhaps time to redo or finish tasks. When you can look at your anger more objectively and think of ways you might help prevent a frustrating situation, you'll find that a lot of the "umph" in your emotional reaction will dissipate.

Let's look at this same kind of phenomenon happening with a younger child. Let's say you just got up from the table to get something, and when you sit down you notice your baby pouring milk from her sippy cup onto the floor. You instantly get angry and yell at her to stop. You might grab the cup away. You might angrily say, "Don't do that!"

Instead, take the time to see why you're so upset and if someone had reacted to you that way in the past. Were you punished (physically, through words or tone of voice) for exploring your environment, even when innocent curiosity caused a disturbance you hadn't planned? Respectful parenting strategies allow you to look at the situation differently. If a baby takes her sippy cup and pours milk on the floor, she is not being "bad." She may simply be exploring the world around her, seeing what happens when the cup is held upside down. She already knows what happens if it's right side up or if it's tipped to her mouth, but she doesn't know what happens if it's upside down.

If her action is met with a simple, "Now you know what happens when you put your cup upside down. I'll get a sponge and clean it up. If you want to drink your milk, you'll need to hold it the other way." She probably won't do it again, because you haven't made it a big exciting thing by getting all upset about it.

Babies and small children like to see they have an effect on the world. When you blow up over small things, they see, feel, and hear the physical sensation of how they manipulated their little world. Your emotional reactions can be exciting to them. They're more likely to reproduce those exciting things again. Their behavior, in and of itself, is not malicious or "manipulative" in a negative sense. Your overcharged emotional reaction is probably more responsible for any repetitive performance. So when you stay calm, the situation loses its appeal and it's not likely to happen again. You can defuse a situation (including your reactions to the baby's actions) by looking at it positively, commenting on it for what it is, and getting on with your day, rather than becoming embroiled in a no-win power struggle.

Your parents probably disciplined you using a punishment that they felt "fit the crime." What crime? The crime of being a curious baby? The crime of being an active toddler? The crime of being a questioning 2-year-old? Unfortunately, "discipline" has often been coupled with shame. Parents can, unwittingly, through their tone of voice, portray a sense of shame. Messages like "You didn't pick up your toys" can be said with cutting sarcasm, venomous anger, or disgusted shamefulness by parents who are intolerant of age-appropriate forgetfulness. It can also be said angrily by parents who are caught up in their own personal histories and are about to choose a punishment for such a "crime."

The words, "You didn't pick up your toys" can also be said matter-of-factly, in a way that simply describes the behavior. A pleasant dialogue with problem solving, where you're both on the same team rather than in a one-up adversarial relationship, can follow. You actually invite a calm solution when you use a nonjudgmental approach.

Parents can use punishment as a shortcut to getting something done. Talking takes longer. Examining where your reactions come from, asking yourself if you want to be stuck in old, automatic, unconsciously motivated behaviors that hurt you and your child takes longer. Asking yourself if your current behavior is what you want to be passing along to your children takes time and energy. Coming up with new options takes time and energy. Trying them out and involving a small child takes time and energy. Refocusing and viewing your child's actions more positively takes time and energy. And lastly, behaving differently as a parent takes time and energy. Why do it? Because when you do, you feel better and so do your children. You provide your children with a healthy legacy. You help them develop a strong healthy self-esteem. You give them a better start in their world. You make it easier for them to live up to their full potential in their life and give them the tools necessary to be healthy human beings in this world.

Modeling Punishment

In past generations, parents often used "hitting" or "spanking" as their main form of discipline. If we think about it, isn't it ridiculous to assume we can "teach" children that a behavior is not acceptable by hitting or spanking them? A parent may hurt a child enough (by spanking them) to have them not do something out of fear, but that's called learned fear, not learning acceptable options.

When you remember that the most powerful way we learn is by copying what we've seen, by hitting, a parent is actually teaching her child a different lesson than she is setting out to teach. The lessons being taught are that hitting and intimidation—especially those younger, smaller, and less able to defend themselves—are okay. Given this perspective, when a large adult hits a small child, that's about as disrespectful as you can be. The child can't hit you back. You're much too big. The child can't "defend himself" by telling the parent to go to his room or that he's out of control. A so-called "simple spanking" can develop into a beating when a parent can't control her unleashed emotions. Abusive parents usually were abused themselves and find themselves operating on automatic pilot once certain remembered emotions are triggered. This time they may be on the giving instead of receiving end, but their fury has its own path. It makes sense that hitting ought to be eliminated as an option for parents.

It's true that children need and crave limits. Respectful parenting does not advocate a free-for-all. It does, however, advocate a humanistic, calm, thoughtful, negotiated approach. It empowers children because they're aware of the consequences before they do something, and as they get older they help decide their own consequences, so they can make conscious choices rather than submitting out of fear and intimidation.

What the Parents Say

Cindy: Somehow, we had gotten into it one day. My daughter and I were just arguing. I don't even remember the specifics, but I know I was in her room. All of a sudden in the middle of "Yes, you will" and "No, I won't," I looked around me. I mean, there I was at 35, and there she was at 2. Only her behavior made sense for her age, and mine . . . was my mother's. I didn't like it when she did it to me when I was a kid, and I didn't like it when I saw myself doing it to my child.

I apologized and told my daughter there was really nothing wrong with what she was doing, but that I didn't like what I was doing or saying, so I was going to take a time-out, sit on my bed, and think for a couple of minutes. I asked her if she'd be okay and play safely for a few minutes while I went to my room. I left both doors open so I could hear her playing (our rooms were only about 15 feet apart). She said okay.

A few seconds later, I heard the patter of her little feet as she walked down the hall to my room. I was thinking I could have used at least a full minute to myself, but there she was. She pulled over her stool, climbed onto the bed and stroked my back saying, "It's okay, Mommy."

She was comforting me, as I've comforted her so often. By loving my daughter, I had taught her how to love me. My anxiety instantly cleared out of my body. I gathered her in my arms and hugged her tightly. I thanked her for her comfort and told her I was feeling better. By the end of the hug we were ready to play and enjoy each other again.

Stephanie: When my daughter was 11 months old, something happened that could have been really bad. It was one of those nights where she was overtired and had been whining a lot, all through dinner. I guess my husband's nerves were shot because when she threw her fork on the floor, he reached over and slapped her hand. She looked up at him and said, "Daddy no hit. You hit, I hit." And she slapped him. He looked at me bewildered. He was silent for a while. I took over parenting as he got up from the table and excused himself.

I had been upset when I saw him hit her. It was the first time. We had talked about spanking quite a bit and couldn't agree on it. I kept saying no, under no circumstances, but he thought when a child was really acting up and had been for a while, and all else failed, that a spanking was perfectly fine. I didn't like it that we didn't agree, but I couldn't convince him. I guess I had been hoping, rather naively, that we'd never encounter the situation. So when it happened, and she was so young, I was pretty upset. But before I could even intervene she had stood up for herself.

When he and I talked about it later (after she was in bed) he said he had realized from her words and actions that she was right. If he could hit her, she could hit him. He said he had known at that second that it was wrong for a parent to hit a child, and he wouldn't be doing it again. The next morning, first thing, he talked to her and apologized for hitting her. He told her that he had learned from her that hitting wasn't okay for anybody. They agreed on a "no-hitting rule" for everyone in our family.

Another feature of respectful parenting involves being real with your children. Being honest, caring, and straightforward. Some of the examples you have just read illustrate this point. For instance, a parent can say to a child, "I'm confused. I'm not sure how to handle this. Give me a few minutes." Or a parent can say, "I don't like how I'm behaving with you right now. I need a time-out." This kind of behavior teaches your children honesty. They learn all people make mistakes, and it's easier to admit mistakes than to carry through with behaviors or words that don't feel comfortable. Your children are also learning how to assess and reevaluate what they're doing and saying, and if necessary, change midway.

Remember that old expression, "To err is human"? But how often do we see people stuck in behaviors they don't like because their false pride won't let them backtrack and say "I'm sorry—I've made a mistake" and change. Children of parents who are real see their parents with real pride, rather than false save-face pride. Being human isn't so scary to these children. Rather than feeling insecure about changing their minds, they learn that they can make mistakes and learn from them. They will know they need time to make healthy decisions. And they will know they can do things differently and think of more options. All these lessons result in them feeling more confidence in their abilities to cope with difficult situations.

Helping Your Child with Transitions

Transitions are times and circumstances that change you and your child's routine. There are big transitions and little transitions. Some children love changes and find them exciting while others prefer things to stay the same. It often doesn't matter whether a first or second transition is big or small, it still involves change. How you handle the first few transitions with your child may set the stage for how he handles changes later in life. Transitions may involve: mom is home full-time, mom is not home full-time. It may be: we have been living here, now we're going to be living there. It could be: I used to nurse, now I'm not. Your child's first transition may be: my mommy and daddy used to live together, and now they are going to live in two houses.

No matter what the nature or degree of the change, remember, you are judging from your adult world view. To your child, who is learning to deal with the newness of life in general, a change may be taken in stride if you help her through it. On the other hand, it may be frightening to her if she perceives and feels things being very different and no one is taking the time to introduce the new ideas to her. She will not feel "safe" unless you help her react to the changes. Children will often follow your lead. If you are calm and prepared, they will feel safer and often mirror your behavior in a transition. If you plan things well and make the necessary preparations, going through transitions smoothly is just another learning experience for both of you, no matter how old you are and no matter how old your child is.

It is also important to keep in mind how a child's perspective is different than an adult's. To a very young child, if something is packed into a box (for an anticipated move), it doesn't exist anymore. He may mourn the loss of a favorite toy. As an adult, you know it will get unpacked "soon," but it is difficult for a child to get the concept of "soon"—he only knows now or never. Thus, if you are moving or changing rooms around in your house and your child begins to get agitated, you'll need to stop and reassure him that this is for now, not forever. If your family is moving, it's a good idea to pack your child's room last so that your child enjoys the least disruptions possible.

Sometimes parents forget and think that because they have helped prepare a child for an imminent change, once they are into or through the change, everything *should* be fine. Then the parent gets frustrated, annoyed with their child if it isn't "fine" with him, or they second-guess themselves, wondering what they didn't do right to better prepare their child. As the parent, you may not have done anything wrong. You may simply have a child who perceives change as different and scary rather than something else she does in a day. Until you're partway through a large change in your child's routine, you really won't be able to predict how your child will relate to the process. And change is a process. There are the preparations beforehand, the change itself, and then settling into a new routine.

For instance, if you've been a stay-at-home parent and you are returning to the work force, there will be a number of steps you'll take to do that, creating an environment full of change: (a) you will be looking for a job or talking to your employer about a return date; (b) you'll be mentally adjusting yourself to going back and dealing with adults all day instead of a baby; c) you will begin trying on clothes or taking your baby with you to buy work clothes; (d) you'll begin hunting for suitable day care arrangements—in your home, in someone else's home, or at a day care center—which will include many telephone calls and personal visits; (e) you'll bring your child to visit for a short time and gradually increase the time at the day care setting; and (f) you'll eventually have your actual first day back to work itself. But the transition isn't over then. You still have to deal with your reaction to the changes, your child's reaction, what happens the first time your child is sick and needs to come home, and whether you or your partner will pick her up. Then there are often those psychological struggles you thought you'd sail through: what do you do with (a) your guilt at leaving your child; (b) your guilt at enjoying your work; (c) your trepidation that someone else can *really* provide your baby with the love you had been providing; or maybe the (d) guilt that you're a little relieved to be among adults for part of your time; or (e) resentment that you have to work when all that is important to you is being a full-time mother to your baby and you can't have that one wish because of economic realities. Any larger transition in life will be similar, with a number of things taking place over a period of time before and after the actual change itself. You will need to be sensitive to yourself, your partner, and your child throughout the entire period.

Helping your child through transitions is a lot like performing a balancing act with various shaped objects, because there are so many different factors involved. You have to take into account preparing yourself, preparing your child, timing, dealing with your own personal background about changes, dealing with transitions as a family process—as well as how to give and get support throughout the process so you're not drained of your own creative energy. That's a lot to keep track of at once.

In preparing your child, you'll want to talk to her about the impending change, walk her through it as best you can, and then hope she makes the transition as smoothly as possible. It helps if you can stay physically and emotionally close to your child during the change itself, so you can support your child through any rough spots she encounters along the way.

Strategies

- **Keep in mind your child's ability to cope with changes when planning transitions.**

- **Slow down the process so you can all be rational and decide things with a first-things-first strategy base.**

- **As you introduce the actual transition to your child, look, listen, and feel your child's reactions with a willingness to compromise if possible.** If a job opportunity has you moving in two months and you know you can't pass up the opportunity, you can still let your young child in on the decisionmaking process.

- **Prepare your child for the transition by introducing your child slowly to new things.** Engage and encourage your child to participate however he can.

- **Remember that you are an adult and change may be difficult for you in spite of lots of coping tools you have. Remember that your child doesn't have all the years of life experience that you have.** Be gentle and bring him along with you rather than pulling him into place.

Easing Your Child Through Transitions

Communicate

Some people believe small children (under 2 or 3) don't need to be brought in on the change process. They believe small children can't understand or don't notice changes happening around them. In respectful parenting, we assume children will be picking up enough cues on their own—noticing that change is in the air—that they deserve and are entitled to explanations as soon as your behavior and attitudes concerning the change spill into their world.

If babies, toddlers, and especially 2-year-olds aren't included in the process, they'll make their own interpretations based on their sense of your changed energies, attitudes, and attentions. They'll know something in their world is amiss. When they're left out, they're more likely to develop fear and anxiety about why their world is suddenly different and what the differences they are sensing might mean. If you're role modeling silence, they'll probably take their cues from you. Instead of asking, "Mommy what's wrong?" or "Daddy angry?" they'll act out their fears.

During transitional times, you're often overworked and stressed from trying to cope with your "normal" responsibilities as well as the added tasks and emotional baggage involved with the change. So, when your child acts out, you may not be able to react in as patient and understanding a way as usual. Couple that with any unresolved "stuff" you have about going through changes in your early life and how your own parents dealt with it and you really have a negative set-up. You get more upset. Your child is more scared. She acts out. You get angry at her. She is more scared. She acts out more . . . and a downward spiral can be set in motion.

On the other hand, if you role model openness about what the whole family is experiencing and why, your child will learn that it's safe to ask questions and ask for support. He won't have to demand reassurance in an indirect way that might not get him the kind of energy (loving) he is looking for.

Stay Calm

When you are respectfully parenting your child, you two are very close. You are intuitively connected to each other. Your child will therefore be aware of what you feel. He will be picking up on your mood shifts and swings. In order to help your baby feel safe when you are with him, you need to be as much your old self as possible. This way your baby knows external changes may be happening, but his mom and dad are still the same, so he's safe. That will help your baby tremendously and will be an important lesson in the differences between inside and outside changes and how you can feel stable when changes are happening around you.

Time It Right

Along with advocating openness, you need to consider one qualifier: timing. Timing is extremely important. You'll need to remember that a child's time frame is different from an adult's time frame. If you tell your child too soon, he may have too much time to conjure up all kinds of anxious anticipation. Or he may get impatient and feel like it's never going to happen. If you tell him too late, then he's already picked up cues from your behavior that he hasn't been able to interpret, and his behavior and yours will be a mismatch. That's a setup for mutual discomfort until you straighten out what he *thinks* is happening from what is happening.

There's no set rule for knowing exactly when to tell your child about upcoming events. It depends upon her developmental abilities, how she copes with change, and the upcoming change itself. The key is to let her know as much as she can handle as soon as you feel like your emotional or physical energy is changing and impacting your child's schedule. Share the process with her, so she's not reacting to perceived differences without an accurate context to understand what's happening in her world. Even if she doesn't understand all the concepts, she will feel safer if "secrets" aren't in the air.

One mother I worked with was trying to decide when to tell her child that she was pregnant. She didn't want to tell her until she was "showing" because, even then, four months would be an eternity for a 2½ year old. The parents decided to wait.

Unfortunately, nature didn't cooperate. During her second month, this mom experienced a large drop in her energy level. She needed to rest and nap. Her daughter was anxious. "Mommy sick? Mommy get better? Why Mommy not play?" became her refrain.

After discussing the pros and cons, this mother decided to tell her daughter that she was really quite healthy and that she had a baby seed growing inside her. She reminded her daughter of all the seeds they had planted in the spring and how they had to wait for the flowers to grow. Since this mother had had a couple of miscarriages already, she didn't want her daughter to have too much false hope, so she added a caveat to the metaphor. She reminded her daughter that a lot of the seeds they planted had not grown into flowers and they couldn't be sure this baby seed would become a real live baby. Like with the seeds, they had to be patient.

Perhaps because this little girl had experienced beginning the garden and waiting, her mother's explanation sufficed. Her anxiety lowered, and she was content to play near her mother when she was resting.

Sympathize

If you take the time to think and act using respectful parenting techniques when your child is acting out, you'll be able to gather your anxious child in your arms and reassure him that, "Yes, things feel different, and Mommy and Daddy are still here with you." You'll view your child's behavior as his attempt to get something from you that will make his world feel safe again. He probably first tried a more subtle approach that you didn't notice. Now, in desperation, he's trying something that's more likely to get your attention. An understanding and supportive response, assuming a positive intent on his part, would be the respectful parenting way to cope. Old-style parenting would assume a stance of anger toward the child for adding more of a burden to your mind by being "oppositional."

If you are able to stay present with your children during these times, it will initially involve more emotional and physical energy, but it will smooth the transition—thus saving you energy in the long run. Yes, you have to take care of all the adult details involved in whatever change you're going through and you have to be there with extra reassurance, love, and playtime for your child even if you're scared, anxious, and stressed yourself.

Perhaps the hardest part is accepting how powerless you may feel watching your child going through these transitions. You can help smooth a transition by preparing your child, but ultimately, it's your children who go through the transition themselves, making their own choices, which you'll react to as respectfully and honestly as possible. Their emotions can run the gamut from delight and excitement to discomfort and downright misery. Your children will definitely take cues from you, so if you validate and respect their feelings, and show them how you're handling your own, they won't feel as lost. Your reactions will rub off on them. The more you respect their reactions, the more you validate their feelings, the faster life will settle down.

When Nothing Else Works

When this scenario doesn't work so smoothly, it will help if you realize that after properly preparing your child, after sympathizing until you're losing your patience, after hugs and loving hasn't worked, the best thing you can do is let your small child know that you have faith in them and their ability to cope. Assume then that the transitional roughness will smooth out and life will be okay again.

It's imperative to add that before you take the "faith" tact (that everything really is okay), make sure your child's complaints or uncomfortable feelings are not based in reality. In other words, make sure there isn't something "real" going on in the new situation that is causing your child's discomfort. Children do get physically abused, emotionally traumatized, and sexually molested. Unfortunately, you can't blindly rule out these possibilities. When you suspect that any of these things has happened, make several unannounced visits at various times. Talk over your fears with someone else who is more familiar with the situation. If you're still not feeling secure about your child's safety, please call in outside assistance to investigate.

If all seems to be going well, then you can breath a sigh of relief. Try to remind yourself that all life transitions involve emotional changes. It's the degree that varies. See if you can view your child's first transition as the biggest of his life, because it's the *only* one he's experienced so far. For that matter, his first few changes may seem monumental and scary because he doesn't have previous experience to draw from. For instance, to you, a new babysitter may not be a big deal. You've interviewed the sitter. You feel comfortable. You feel safe leaving your child. You're looking forward to going out and having an adult night out. So what's the big deal for your child?

You've done all the right things. Example: You're leaving your child with a babysitter for the first time. You've talked about it in advance with your small child, but not so far in advance as to cause too much anticipation on your child's part. You know the person is safe. You know you'll only be gone a few hours. You're okay—so why isn't your child?

Keep in mind: your mind is at ease. Your emotions are in place. You may even be a little sad at leaving your baby for the first time, or the first time in a long time, but you know that's a natural response. Your child's perspective is different. She sees you leaving. She feels your different energy. She sees you leaving her with a stranger. She knows you've talked to her, but how long will you be gone?

If you sympathize for a little while, but then get uncomfortable with her feelings because you couldn't make it better for her, give yourself a time-out. Consider the scenario from your child's perspective. Sense her increasing discomfort, and try to identify what it is and where it's coming from. You don't want to make changes uncomfortable and scary. Change is an integral part of life and if your child gets set up at an early age to dislike changes, life is going to be difficult for her.

Take some deep breaths. Go back ready to be with your child, talk soothingly, and accept where she's at. She deserves your acceptance and respect for her situation, even if it's inconvenient for you. You can't always make it better. Sometimes feelings have to stick around for a while, even uncomfortable ones. That's a real part of life.

Try to see the bigger picture. Instill a sense of delight with change through your words and actions. Don't be afraid of your children's emotions. Don't try to will them away. Guide them through the process, explaining, planning, looking at the brighter side, validating the not-so-bright side. Your goal during your children's changes and transitions is to be encouraging, yet not pushy. Validating, yet not reinforcing their fears. Hopeful, yet realistic, until whatever change they are dealing with is okay with them.

Some Common Transitions

In previous chapters, I have dealt with developmental milestones that are also transitions for children and parents, such as potty training or stopping the use of a pacifier. Following are some other common transitions in children's lives.

Beginning Day Care or Preschool

At some point, usually before kindergarten and often anywhere from 6 weeks to 3 years of life, a child will begin spending some time in day care or a preschool. It is difficult to predict how your child will react, especially if this is your child's first major transition. Planning and preparation for you and your child will go a long way. Begin by making phone calls to friends and asking them where they take their children and what programs they suggest. After interviewing directors about availability and price, you will probably want to know about the philosophy and contents of their program and about the training and background of their staff. If this information "fits" with your hopes for the kind of program you want your child exposed to, go on your own the first time to check it out.

If your visit is successful and you like what you see, then you're ready to take your child for a short time during the day when he is alert, aware, and interactive. Don't take him when he's hungry or tired. You could tell him that you've checked this place out and you really like it and you're wondering how he likes it. Even if he's preverbal, somehow your thoughtfulness will come through. When you are there for your first visit, make it a short one—20 to 30 minutes, tops. That way your child won't feel overwhelmed, especially if he's used to being home alone with you. Afterward, if your child is verbal, ask him what he liked about the place and if there was anything he didn't like. Take his concerns seriously and address them individually.

Go back a few times before enrolling your child. You might extend each visit a little longer so your child gets used to being there for longer time periods. Make it a fun, exciting change. Talk about how proud you are of how beautifully your child is growing up and how much fun you know he will have with the other children.

After beginning the program, continue to take your child's feelings seriously. Get the staff involved if necessary. It's also a good idea to make surprise visits to see what is happening when the program staff does not expect you to be around. You can do this even if your child is not complaining about anything. If your child is having nightmares or reacting very differently than before you placed him in the day care program, it is especially important to check out the program at unexpected times to make sure your child is being treated well.

Some children may have a difficult time adjusting no matter what you do. I remember our day care center staff saying that if day care is not introduced before a child is 9 months old, that child will have a much more difficult adjustment. Before the age of 9 months, it's a relatively easy transition, because it is what the child knows. It feels natural to him to be dropped off. Each child is a unique individual, however, and will react in his or her own way.

If your time for day care is delayed and your child is a few years old, in addition to visiting the center, you can try to find some books where children go to day care and enjoy it. These would be very helpful to read to your child.

As with any transition, the more you prepare, the better idea your child has, the more familiar she is with the change, the easier it will be on her. In addition, if your child senses that you feel good, that you are comfortable with the place, that you believe it is safe, and that you have been careful in your decisionmaking about the day care situation, your child will feel your ease and most probably "copy" it.

Separation or Divorce

Having a child marks the important transition from "couple" to "family." It can be a difficult transition because of all the additional responsibilities and challenges both new parents must face in a sleep-deprived state. If you and your partner have been "playmates" before becoming "parents," sometimes one or both of you have trouble buckling down and facing the responsibilities parenting involves. Tensions can easily build around who is doing what and who is not. Tempers flare. Blame is placed and denied. And all of a sudden having this wonderful human being (the baby) that was supposed to bring you both closer together has torn you apart. It is impossible to predict how you and your partner will relate to all the changes inherent in becoming parents and a family. All the necessary changes affect the dynamics between two people tremendously!

I would highly recommend that if you're having trouble in your marriage, please seek help quickly from a marital or family therapist. Don't wait until there is so much water under the bridge that divorce seems to be the easiest or only answer. Remember, you may successfully divorce your partner, but you will have to see and interact with your partner for the rest of your baby's life. Regardless of whether your relationship with your partner was troubled, your divorce will have a far-reaching emotional impact on your child's life for years to come.

During the first couple of years of life, a child's main task is building trust and establishing a basic level of trust in himself and others, to the point where he knows, on an unconscious level, he can rely on a family team. If a family is torn apart when a child is very young, this basic human need for trust can remain un(der)developed. As a child grows into adolescence and adulthood, he will often experience some of the following problems: lower self-esteem; problems communicating with people close to him; problems expressing his feelings openly; problems with perseverance—knowing how to problem solve and stick with difficult things (since he hasn't seen it at home); and problems establishing and maintaining a long-term intimate relationship.

Judith Wallerstein reported results from her 25-year follow-up study of children from divorced families in California at a one-day conference on divorce, in Denver, Colorado, on October 20, 2000. The complete results can be found in her new book *The Unexpected Legacy of Divorce: A 25 Year Landmark Study.* Of the grown children from this study, 25 years later, 40% of the adult children she interviewed had or wanted children, while 60% felt strongly that they were not going to have children. Those interviewed often remembered the events surrounding the divorce with tears, as if the events occurred yesterday. They described not only losing their "family" but also often losing a main caretaker, as their mom had to go back to school or to work full-time and her energies were largely taken up elsewhere. As one 5-year-old initially told Ms. Wallerstein, "I need a new mommy. The old mommy went away."

There are some circumstances in which divorce is a necessary solution. But in many, it may be avoided by learning how to communicate, negotiate, and problem-solve. If you come from a divorced family, remember, you don't really have a template or model of how to do an adult partnership, how to work things through to a useful solution that will not be 50-50 every day or in every situation, but one that "works" over time. Partnership skills can be learned. Get help to avoid separation and divorce if at all possible.

If you can't avoid divorce, remember, the most important goal for you and your partner needs to be what is in the best interests of your child. This can be accomplished if you can set up two homes where your child knows he or she is loved and safe. A wonderful book that can help you is *Mom's House, Dad's House* by Isolina Ricci (see Other Resources list in back).

The latest research on children and divorce show that quality time with each parent is more important than quantity time.[1] It also appears that the transitions between households is the most potentially stressful time for children. When parents get along during these transitions, the children do well. If parents argue, exhibit anxiety, or ooze disgust toward the other parent, the children suffer emotionally and may act out their sadness or anger at being put in the middle. In other words, there seems to be a direct correlation between how well parents get along with each other postdivorce and how well their children do emotionally in the short run and the long run.

Minimizing all fighting, accusations, and legal battles is *essential* to your child's healthy development and long-term mental health. In other words, parents should not "talk bad" about the other parent within ear shot or possible ear shot of their children. Visits ought to be encouraged between both parents and their children, even if the custodial parent has ill feelings toward the former spouse. Both parents need to encourage a loving relationship with the other parent even though they have chosen not to live together anymore.

Sometimes parents get into accusing each other of "neglect" (or worse) if they do not parent in the same manner. Parents can make overt accusations or they can quietly ooze, roll their eyes, and give their children other indications of their general dislike/disgust of the other parent. This kind of behavior puts the children in the middle of an adult battle zone, a place you don't want your child to be stuck. It's like being a ping pong ball in the middle of a particularly competitive and brutal game. It hurts and, as a child, you can't win. Taking sides produces guilt and loss and staying in the middle involves pain from both ends. Well-meaning parents who want to "prove" they are the "better" or "more responsible" parent harm their child in their attempts to prove their superiority. A child needs the love of *both* parents and is legally entitled to both parents, regardless of whether the parents no longer want to be married.

Even when custodial battles are not an issue, children may be harmed by lengthy court proceedings. Children do not escape continuous court battles, regardless of whether they have been informed about court dates. Somehow it's in the air, because children pick up a lot. I've never met a child whose parents were battling a long, drawn-out set of legal suits and countersuits who did not know his or her parents were embroiled in a costly and frustrating battle. These children feel terrible; they are often afraid it's their fault, that they said something that brought on the parental upset, and they tend to try to behave in ways that will minimize the risk of further courtroom battles, like clamming up and not saying anything.

One exception to the rule of encouraging postdivorce contact would be a parent who was violent to his or her spouse or children during the marriage. Supervised visits may be appropriate, but you should seek the help of an experienced therapist to determine the appropriate amount and type of contact, and to offer your child very necessary counseling. Counseling helps a child refrain from repeating, either as a perpetrator or another victim, the violent pattern he or she has experienced or witnessed over the years.

Overall, the most important lesson here for new parents is to work through problems in as peaceful a way as possible. If your marital problems seem to be escalating, get help before you give up, throw in the towel, and call a lawyer. Engaging in therapy and learning communication and problem-solving skills is a lot less expensive, emotionally and financially, than going through a divorce. If divorce cannot be avoided, therapy can again help that process proceed as smoothly as possible. Parents often engage in therapy themselves but think their children will be fine. "Once the tension is over, they'll bounce back" is a common refrain. The latest research indicates the opposite is true. Your children may "look fine" but that is often because of their valiant attempts to take care of you and not cause you (the parent) further distress. Please don't be fooled by your children being good actors and trying to cope. If you see them having trouble forming or maintaining friendships any time between preschool and adolescence, get them some help.

There is an expression I read someplace that can apply to parents with parenting differences, "We won't always see eye to eye, but we can see heart to heart." Respect each other's differences instead of making value judgments. It can go a long way toward avoiding separation and divorce and if necessary, it can also go a long way to respecting differences postdivorce.

Moving

In our current, highly mobile society, many families will be moving at least once before their child is in kindergarten. Moves may be family motivated or job related. Regardless of the impetus for such a move, many factors will be similar. You will all be leaving the stability of a home and community you are familiar with. You may be moving to a place where you do not have a support network. A good real estate agent can help a lot. They can introduce you to organizations or activities in the new locale that can make your transition easier. Many community churches sponsor "Mom's Day Out" programs a day or two a week, so when you arrive you can have some adult days to unpack or explore.

As soon as you know a move is imminent, before the "for sale" sign goes up in your front yard, your child needs to be brought into the picture. Age appropriate books such as *Moving House,* by A. Civardi, are fun ways to introduce the change. If you are visiting a new town, spend part of the day looking at houses or apartments and spend part of the time in a park or children's museum so your child gets to see how much fun this new place will be.

Pictures of your new town and/or home will help during the packing phase. You can make a little photo album of your "moving adventure" from start to finish.

The most important thing is to ask your child for input wherever possible, like which house he likes the best and why, and which room she'd like for a bedroom. If you're eating out a lot during the process, ask your child what she wants to eat and go to a restaurant where she'll get her favorite (comfort) foods. Moving can be experienced as a family adventure.

What the Parents Say

In the following examples, parents dealt with changes as just another thing families were going to do together or as a fun family adventure. You'll see how small children take their parents' leads. Transitions began to be viewed as interesting, problem-solving situations rather than onerous tasks.

Starting at Day Care

> **Sarah:** My hardest transition with my child so far was when I dropped him off at day care for the first time. He was 4 months old. He was only going to be there a few hours a day, four days a week. I was even going to be able to visit and

nurse him halfway through his day, three of the four days. We had visited the day care center several times the week before for a few hours. I had talked to him about needing to go back to work and how he'd be at the day care center while I worked.

I thought I had accepted reality—I needed to work and he needed to be in day care. I knew in my heart and mind this was a good day care center and he'd get good loving care from the caregivers. Yet, as I dropped him off, I had a lump in my throat as big as Mount Everest. He was fine. I hugged him and reassured him that I'd be back soon. Then I put him on the floor, tummy down, near the other infants. He raised his head and looked around with interest. As I said good-bye and walked away, I watched his reactions carefully. He tracked me with his eyes and he was still fine.

I stood outside the door for a couple of minutes to make sure he wasn't going to have a delayed reaction to me leaving. I swear I would have torn back in there and grabbed him if I had heard him crying. He didn't. I knew he was attached to me. I could see he had a healthy sense of security. He knew intuitively he was safe and I'd be back. I felt pleased and proud that he was taking my leaving so well. Yet there I was, in the hallway, unable to leave, my eyes filling with tears, my chest tearing itself up. I was surprised by how strongly I felt.

I shed a few tears each of the four days that first week after I dropped him off. My office was only one mile from the day care center, so I didn't cry a lot because I had to be composed when I arrived at work. But each day, a few tears slipped slowly down my cheeks as I felt poignant pangs because I was missing being with my child full-time.

He, on the other hand, was easy-going all week. He smiled and cooed when I came to nurse him. And smiled when I left. One of the caregivers always took him from my arms into her arms to help him with the transition of my leaving and it always worked.

His first transition in life was a positive, easy experience for him. And for me too. I learned from him. I learned that he's a pretty easy-going kid. He has a strong sense of himself and a strong sense of inner security. I'm assuming being nursed whenever he asked, being held whenever he asked, and being loved a lot by his father and mother during those first four months at home helped instill his inner sense of security and comfort. I'm sure some of it was a terrific mix of the best genes his father and I had to offer. And I had prepared him well.

I also learned that my son's transitions are transitions for me as well. I had known he'd need preparation, but I was so used to the fact that I do change well, I hadn't anticipated my own needs and reactions. I had definitely underestimated the power of our first major transition on me. From that experience, I learned to better anticipate my needs during times of change.

Cathy: When my son's caregiver had a baby, my son was gentle and responsive when she asked. He could even play quietly when she told him her baby was sleeping and needed him to be quiet so the baby could stay asleep. I think she had always done such a good job of making him feel special, he was happy to do something for her. Because he was so close to her, I worried when we moved about 40 minutes away, and he'd need new day care arrangements . . . I didn't know how he would adjust to her loss.

I think it may have been a little easier for him because we were building a new home and we'd often go see it and how it was progressing. He started getting excited about it, so the move itself and the new house weren't a surprise to him. I also think losing her was somewhat softened by our excitement about the move, his anticipation, and our talking about how different and fun life was going to be living in the mountains.

After a couple of weeks in the new house he said, "We should go see [the caregiver] and [her son]." We'd call and she'd talk to him. Sometimes that was enough for him. He felt like he had visited, and he'd drop his requests to actually go there. But other times he was more insistent and we'd go and visit. She'd still make him feel really special asking about his new house and new friends . . . I was glad it was only a 40-minute drive, so it hasn't had to be a clean break. He's kind of eased out of it.

I've taken time off from work, so he hasn't had to establish himself with a new day care provider. I'm also glad he feels comfortable enough to express himself and say he misses her and wants to talk or visit. I've encouraged him to express himself, and it's nice to see that he can, especially softer feelings like missing for a little boy...So it's been a pretty easy transition. I don't know what it would have been like if we hadn't been able to visit her occasionally.

Sylvia: My older son was only a toddler when I found out I was pregnant again. As soon as I started talking about the new baby, I referred to it as his new baby instead of Mommy's new baby. I talked about other children he knew who had babies in their family and stressed how lucky they were. I talked about the new baby I had had when I was growing up, and how that baby grew up to be his aunt (whom he loves). I pointed out babies on the street and reminded him he'd have one of those soon. We liked looking at old baby pictures and videos of when he was a baby. I  explained how babies at first can't do anything for themselves, they can't talk, walk, crawl, sit up, or hold toys, so it would be great if he wanted to hold a toy for the baby. I'd explain the different stages he went through as a baby when we were looking at the photo album...I wanted to establish for him how big he was and how much he could do, so he didn't feel like the new baby was taking his place. I had always told him how proud I was of him, but when I was pregnant I would say things about how proud I was about all he could do and tried to really zero in on any new accomplishments he was making.

I was lucky because we had friends who had babies we could spend time with, but if we hadn't, I think I would have rented one of those video baby care films to show him how he could help with the baby. I also tried to help him understand that babies don't stay babies forever, and soon enough they'd be able to play together.

I let my son help me pick out some new rattles and clothes for the baby. He really enjoyed helping me fix up a new room for the baby. He was given the choice of picking out some of his toys and stuffed animals to give to the baby, if he wanted, which he enjoyed doing.

We played with dolls and stuffed animals often, practicing giving them loves and having them give him gentle hugs. I gave him lots of gentle loves and hugs too, knowing I wanted to prepare him for being loving and tender without having to use words or needing to stop him once the baby arrived. I gave him lots of praise when he was loving with his dolls or animals. In preparation for the birth itself, I brought him to the hospital where I'd be and he was able to see other newborn babies in the nursery. We discussed over and over again, as the date approached, exactly what would be happening and where he'd stay while I was giving birth, and that he'd get to come visit as soon as the baby was born.

After our new baby's birth he was able to visit within an hour... When he held the baby with such delight, I was thrilled and told him so. I also added, "He's looking at you. I think he likes you." The nurse took a photo of him holding the baby. It's still one of his prized possessions. He was excited about taking the picture to day care and showing his friends and teachers.

When I brought the baby home, I explained that because babies can't talk, they cry when they need things, and together we'd try to figure out what the baby was telling us he needed. I also explained that it took a long time to feed the baby (when it was nursing) but it wouldn't take a long time forever, just until he got bigger. I tried to let my older son make as many decisions as possible, like what his baby brother was going to wear that day, or pick something out for him to look at. I continually tried to stress his abilities and his special place in our family as the oldest child. Sometimes it was a tight balancing act between stressing all he could do and also acknowledging how young he was too, and not expecting too much from him—he was barely out of toddlerhood himself.

One of the more subtle ways I did that was by letting him show people his new brother, instead of me always being the one to show my new baby. When the baby would gaze at him, I'd tell him the baby loved him and wanted to grow up to be like him. A few times he did do things that might hurt the baby, like throwing toys at him instead of giving them to him. I'd explain it was my job to protect the baby, just like I had protected him when he was a baby, and just like I still protected him if I saw him doing something dangerous. And I told him when his behavior was just not acceptable, although I didn't have to do that often.

I'm glad I thought ahead, planned, and made sure my oldest son did not feel dislodged with the birth of his baby brother. He was so young, he easily could have felt forced out, but he naturally took to his new role of big brother. I do think it helped stressing all he could do, and involving him so much. It wasn't so much me with the baby and him being left out, it was us with the baby, us having fun, and when the baby was sleeping, he and I had our different fun with toys the baby couldn't play with.

Dealing with Frustrations

Young children work so hard and at such an incredible pace to learn about the big world around them! Since learning something new is often frustrating, it makes sense that young children will often become frustrated. Your child will need your help to learn how to deal with her emotions and the situations that cause them. You can't prevent these feelings; they come along with the learning process called Life.

There seem to be five basic situations that produce frustration for children between birth and age 3: (1) a basic need not being filled, such as hunger or tiredness; (2) a baby or small child trying to accomplish something he can't physically or developmentally do; (3) overstimulation; (4) too much time engaged in "adult activities" without enough play time or child-centered time; and (5) the "I want it now" frustration, as she begins to learn the difference between needs and wants.

Small children have to learn there are things that don't get addressed exactly as they would like all the time. In other words, they need to learn the art of waiting, and that can be frustrating. Long before your child has words for expressing her frustration, she has nonverbal ways of letting you know "I've had it!" The first and most universal expression infants and babies use is an all-purpose, slightly altered intonation of their basic cry.

Think about situations where you're feeling frustrated, where you're looking for the perfect expression that you can use in front of your small child. You don't want to curse, scream, throw things, or shake someone, yet you're so frustrated you can't think straight. A good cry might be a good release, but adults are too socialized and "mature" to let loose with a good, healing cry. You may also be worried about the effects your crying may have on others around you, so you hold back your tears.

Strategies

- **Remember that teaching patience and the art of waiting takes time and practice.**

- **Look at difficult times as life lessons for you and your child.** You're learning her limits better and she is communicating hers to you and trusting that you will listen.

- **When your child is upset, try to think of reasons that explain the stress and ways that you can lessen the stress.** Don't blame or shame your child.

- **Plan your days around your child's schedule** so that activities occur during times she is normally energetic, and naps and meals can be taken at the usual times.

Unmet Needs

Infants and babies instinctively know that crying is a great release. Besides releasing their built-up tensions, crying often results in someone (often a parent) responding quickly. In respectful parenting, that someone will check out what's happening, soothe the baby, and alleviate the situation. The end result? The baby is no longer feeling uncomfortable. In old-style parenting, the parent might come in and say loudly, "If you don't stop crying, I'll give you something to cry about. Now enough is enough. I'm trying to sleep!"

Babies raised with parents who are being respectful have much less cause for frustration. As soon as they express their needs, the needs are addressed and resolved. You have happier babies and less stressed parents. When babies are "mellow" because their needs are being taken care of, they're genuinely happy and they feel safe and secure. In old-style parenting, where you have regimented feedings and nap times, infants and babies have more opportunities to be frustrated, because their basic needs for food, comfort, and security aren't being met.

Babies who are raised by people using respectful parenting techniques are freer with their expressions of love and appreciation than old-style parented babies. Old-style parenting considered people who responded to their children quickly as *responding on demand*, thereby creating a spoiled child. Respectful parenting views timely responses as *responding to a need*. Responding lovingly to a need perpetuates the family's cycle of gentleness and love.

Jeanne: So far, my baby is only 9 months old, but I deal with his frustrations by picking him up, holding him, and nursing him. It's such an easy simple way to calm him down. And it works every time. So that's really all I've had to develop so far.

Bonnie: I recently had one of those days with my 16-month-old daughter where everything was going wrong for her. She couldn't quite communicate and when she seemed to want something, once she got it, she didn't really want it. You know, one of those days where I just couldn't please her or solve it or anything. I started getting frustrated too. All my attempts fell flat. Finally I brought her into my bedroom and started pounding on my mattress. She looked at me kind of funny, and then as I invited her to pound, she joined right in. At first we both just pounded away, but soon, it turned into a fun thing, as our frustration just kind of melted away. Since then, I've given her a tambourine to use when she's frustrated. And when I hear it going, although noise like that used to bother me, I know she's getting out some frustration, and I feel relieved for her.

Developmental Hurdles

Babies raised with respectful parents experience frustration when they begin to try and accomplish physical feats they can't perform, feats needing the practice of smaller steps leading up to the whole. Walking is a good example. For most babies, learning to walk is a months-long process that involves a lot of falling down and frustrating bumps and bruises. Parents can help them, but sometimes, developmentally, small children aren't quite ready for what they are tackling. That leads to frustration. Lots of talking and soothing hugs help when a child *really* wants to do something and can't yet accomplish the task.

Perhaps it's a baby who has crawled to a baby gate and wants to get past it. The baby can't crawl under the gate, can't go through the gate, and can't quite manage to climb over it. The baby is stuck, emotionally frustrated, and cries. If a parent is utilizing respectful parenting techniques, he will come over to his child immediately to find out what's wrong. What happens?

He picks up his baby, so he can communicate with her more easily. By picking up his baby, he's lifted her clear over the gate where she wanted to be. As her father soothingly asks what's wrong, she feels safe, loved, and secure. If she squirms in his arms, he knows that she was after something on the floor level, or perhaps she's pointing to something on a piece of furniture. By taking cues from his baby, the father is able to provide a satisfying end to her frustrating experience. Everyone is happy again.

Another example of an older child who wants to do something that he just can't physically accomplish comes to mind. It was a situation I encountered with my two-and-a-half-year-old. He *really* wanted to help me tie his shoes. (In truth, he wanted to tie his shoes all by himself, but he'd settle for helping.) When we tried to do it together, he was sometimes able get the first half-knot done, but often he started getting frustrated.

I'd take him in my arms and say something like, "It looks like being able to tie your shoes is important to you right now. I can see you're trying really hard to understand and do what I'm telling you. But you know what? It looks like you're not ready to tie them yet. I know you want to, but physically I don't think you can. And that's fine. There's lots of times where we want to do something we're not yet ready to do. Like you had to learn to crawl, pull yourself up on furniture, and walk along holding on to furniture for months before you could walk all by yourself. Tying shoes is one of those things that takes a while and practice. I hope you can have patience with yourself and wait a while till you're bigger."

I thought I had explained the situation well and hoped my son would understand he just couldn't be expected to tie shoes yet. He wasn't developmentally ready. But he was determined, and he responded with, "But I want to, please show me, we'll practice."

I thought a little and continued, "Even though tying shoes looks easy, because I've been doing it for years, it's really a hard thing to learn. I didn't learn till I was a lot older than you are now. I was almost in kindergarten, and even then it was hard for me to learn. There are some things you have to wait till you're bigger to be able to do. Tying shoes is one of them. We can try every once in a while to see if you're ready, but I don't want you to feel bad over something you're just not able to do yet. Can you understand that?"

"But I'm big now."

"Yes, you are big now, and you'll be getting even bigger. And when you're quite a bit bigger, your fingers and your brain will be much better at tying shoes. I like the way you keep trying and wanting to. One day you'll be able to, but let's put off trying for a while, because it looks like you're getting frustrated and you don't have to. One day this will be much easier and you'll learn without too much frustration. Okay?"

In that situation, I wanted to validate his efforts. He was persistent, and I think persistence is a good quality to reinforce. But persistence in the face of a task that developmentally he *can't* master may lead to unnecessary frustration and feelings of failure. He didn't need that. I also wanted to tell him that he's not the only one who can't master tying shoes at two years of age. It's one of those things older kids get to do.

I used my memories as a reality mirror for him. The other thing I did, which I recommend, was to look for ways of alleviating the frustrating situation. Since he wanted to help or be able to put his own shoes on, when it was time to get his next pair of shoes, we bought shoes with Velcro closures. With the Velcro closures he could be independent, get his shoes on, be developmentally just where he belonged, and feel good about himself and his accomplishments!

When your child is frustrated in other situations, look for creative solutions. For instance it often helps to take away the stimulus that's producing his discomfort and offer an explanation. Help him through it by talking about what's happening. Face reality and decide if he's ready for the situation he's facing. It's fine to shelve things for later. Life is a series of experiences. Sometimes the timing is right. Sometimes it's wrong.

When you explain to your child that the timing is wrong and that she is feeling frustrated for good reason, she will feel relieved. When she's feeling better, try to explain that she was just challenging herself in a no-win situation. Assure her that you will help her again when she has a chance of successfully accomplishing what she's attempting to accomplish. You'll be modeling appropriate behaviors she can use later in life, when she's faced with situations where she needs more resources than she has on hand. Perhaps she will know how to ask for help when she's an adult rather than attempting the impossible.

There's a link here between knowing your limits, learning to ask for help, putting things off until the timing is better, having the proper resources to accomplish a task, and procrastination. People procrastinate when they're assuming, "I can't do that. It's just too hard. Why tackle it at all?" A respectful parent is not saying, "We'll never do it," or "You'll never do it." A respectful parent is saying, "We'll do it when it's possible," and "We'll try periodically to see if you're ready." Respectful parents teach their child how to cope with difficult tasks and frustrating situations.

Bonnie: Our 2-year-old daughter started saying, "No, no," when we offered her things, and when we withdrew the offer she'd say "Yes, yes." This could go on a few times until we were all confused and frustrated. We realized that with her, it wasn't about the thing itself; the no, no, yes, yes had become a power struggle and a vicious cycle. So when we "got into it" with her, and were in the merry-go-round of "No, no," "Yes, yes," instead of us cycling into frustration with her, we made up a "No, no. Yes, yes," song and made it fun. The song completely defused the power struggle and we all ended up laughing and going on to something else that was more fun.

≈

When my daughter was about 2 ½, she was going through what my husband and I came to call the "I want it, I don't want it" frustration a lot. At first I kept trying to fix it for her. And the result? She just became more frustrated. Finally I found that after a couple of attempts at talking or fixing it, the best thing I could do was recognize that it was her frustration and know that sometimes it's okay for her to be frustrated. After all, frustration is one of those human emotions we all have from time to time. So I would recognize that the object she was venting her frustration on might have little to do with what she was really frustrated about. I'd let her be and let her work it through on her own. Amazingly "it" would just pass, and she'd calm herself down.

Trying to Do Too Much

Toddlers and 2-year-olds often get frustrated because their parents have planned too much in a day, and they develop a good case of stimulation overload coupled with exhaustion. That's not their fault. As a mother who was learning about respectful parenting said, "I can't blame her when she starts acting up in a store after a couple hours of shopping. It's simply her way of telling me I overdid it for her."

When children start losing it in public places, parents ought to tell their child, "Thank you for letting me know you've had enough. Let's go sit someplace quiet" or "Let's get a snack and give each other some good attention for a while" or "Let's just forget all this right now. I'll explain to the salesperson. You and I can go home and get a (nap, snack, quiet time, play time, etc.), which you really seem to need right now."

How different from old-style parenting where a parent would say, "Will you please just behave? What's wrong with you? I don't understand why you're doing this, and I want you to stop immediately!"

When you take the time to look at the situation, you can understand. You probably created the situation by doing at least one of the following: overexposing your child to adult stimuli without providing enough child-centered time, missing a nap, being late for a meal or missing a snack, or ignoring your child's pace and her needs. To ask her to stop "right now" is an unrealistic expectation that will only result in more unhappiness and frustration for everyone. She wants to please you, but can't. Leaving the situation as quickly as possible and understanding her frustration are the first steps toward everyone being able to calm down.

This type of frustration can often be avoided by some forethought and planning. Try to remember that your small child hasn't planned an overstimulating day. He's just along for the ride. You planned the day. He's doing the best he can. If there are consequences you hadn't planned for, who gets to deal with them? You ought to, as understandably and lovingly as possible. Again, walking in your child's shoes for a few minutes, seeing and feeling what it must be like as an overtired, overhungry, or overstimulated 2-year-old will go a long way toward you being able to lovingly take your child out of the situation. Your other alternatives are to be annoyed, disappointed, angry, or furious. Which will it be?

Patience

The last source of frustration for some of the older children in the birth to 3-year age bracket comes when they're learning what I call the art of waiting. As infants and babies, their needs were addressed immediately. As toddlers and 2-year-olds, they are beginning to want some things they don't need to get so quickly. To them, their wants feel as urgent and as important as their needs felt. They need to be taught the difference.

When all they had were basic needs, you addressed them immediately. Since there's no difference to them in how it feels to *want* to stay at a park longer and to *need* to eat, they don't understand why, from their perspective, all of a sudden you're not readily responding. They hear their loving Mommy and Daddy say, "No, we're not going to stay. It's time to leave" or "I can see you really *want* to stay, but it's getting late and we really do have to go now." Even though wants may feel as important to them as needs always have, there are differences. They're going to have to learn the subtle and not-so-subtle differences between needs and wants. It's a difficult lesson at any age, but being exposed to it for the first time is particularly frustrating.

Children going through these lessons also have to get reassurance that Mommy and Daddy will still be there for all their basic needs: comfort,

security, love, food, and sleep. Parents using respectful parenting techniques can help their children learn about these differences. Learning is a
two-way street, with solutions, compromises, and limits.

Parents need to offer solutions that address the child's wants directly,
validate them, understand the immediacy behind them, explain why
they can't be addressed right now, and then follow through with what
the parent says has to happen at that point in time. Sometimes, a parent
will listen to her child's want, rethink her own agenda, and agree to be
more flexible after explaining why (so the child doesn't get the idea Mom
is a total pushover).

In other situations, a parent can listen to the child, rethink the entire
situation, and suggest a compromise. An example would be, "You're
telling me you really want to stay at the park a little longer. Maybe I didn't
give you enough time to get adjusted to the idea of having to leave. I'm
going to give you that time now. Why don't you play for another five
minutes, and then we'll go. When I tell you it's time to go after you have
this extra time, I want you to agree and come willingly. Can you agree to
that?" It's a compromise that holds both of you responsible for the new
agreement.

When you're helping your child learn the art of waiting, it helps to
really listen to his desires and *really consider* them before making a decision. Your child will sense whether you've taken the time to listen and
consider his perspective. When he senses you have, he'll be more willing
to listen to your perspective. Whatever happens after that, it's more likely
to go smoothly when you've respected him by listening and considering
his input, rather than simply sticking to your agenda.

Steve: My 2 ½-year-old son sometimes gets almost frantic for
some toy or thing he wants, but he's saying, "I need this, I
need this! I say to him, "No, you *want* it, and if you'll calm
down, I'll get it for you. It's okay to *want* this, but you don't
really *need* it, like you'd need food if you were hungry, or
something to drink if you were thirsty."

I'm trying to teach him the difference between needs
and wants, and I figure if I can use the examples he gives
me and use the right words, explaining the differences,
he'll get it eventually. His mother and I have agreed

from the beginning that we'd use the right words and concepts for things even if they were beyond his so-called capacity to know exactly what we were talking about, because one day he'd get it and we'd never know when that day was.

It feels like we're respecting his mind, his ability to know, by parenting the way we do. I'm glad it feels natural to both of us. He's a great listener. So far, we can reason with him on just about everything. Sometimes it's seemed like our talking alone has been soothing for him, even if he doesn't understand the words. I like what we're doing with him, and I just think he's the greatest kid.

The Art of Being Human

As you're teaching your child the art of waiting, keep in mind that for his whole life, he hasn't had to wait. Now you're beginning to change the rules he has come to know. He needs your patience and understanding while his world is changing in rather drastic ways. It's no wonder he's frustrated, scared, questioning, and testing.

As one mother said, "I want to respect his attempts at independent thinking, but I'm not used to him saying *no* when I tell him something. He's always been so agreeable. I know he's feeling confident when he says no. I know he knows it's safe. He knows that I won't go away or get angry at him. That's terrific. I've worked hard these last two-and-a-half years so he can feel confident and good about himself. There are times when it's difficult to not get or sound angry because I am angry or at least annoyed with his wants conflicting with mine, and with having to take the time and make the effort to try to get them in sync. It's a balancing act."

"I want him to learn that he can say no. I can get angry, and our world is still safe. He has to learn I still love him and I'll always be there for him, even though I won't always agree with him. When I leave extra time for explanations and remember that's part of what I want to be doing as his parent, then I'm okay. But when I'm rushed or I forget it's worth the extra effort . . . then I can start sounding shrill as I say, 'I know you want to but we just can't right now. Let's go!' Actually, what I'm saying is that we both have to accept that we are both human. "

There is real wisdom in this last quote. The more you can accept your own and your children's humanity, the more you'll find yourself being loving. The more loving you are, the more easily you'll respect and accept their human foibles, including their frustrations, the behaviors that result from their frustrations, and their attempts at independence, however ill-timed they may seem to you. Keep in mind that your frustration and theirs is interwoven. One builds on the other. It's also true that one can deescalate the other.

Slyvia: When my son was about 2½, he was having a rough time one morning. Nothing was seeming right, and he started whining. Before he escalated any more I went over, bent down to his level and asked, "Do you need a Mommy hug?" "Yes," came his reply and we hugged and hugged. When we released each other, he was okay again. It feels so good to do those little loving things that can help him so much.

What Do You Do When Your Strategies Don't Work?

Most of the time your frustrations probably piggyback onto your child. Your frustrations can also come when you're unable to change the situation in front of you or when your expectations of how things "should" be do not match how life is as a parent. Like when your 2-year-old puts her hands on her hips and says things like, "I don't have to do that," or "I'm bigger than you!" or "NO! NO! NO! NO!" These confrontations are exacerbated if you happen to be hungry, tired, distracted, stressed about something else, or overworked. Then instead of keeping your cool, laughing it off, negotiating, walking away, ignoring it, knowing through and through that you don't have to play, or taking a time-out, you may find yourself yelling, crying, whining, screaming, grabbing them, or getting to your child's level and doing such things as sticking out your tongue.

Sometimes, it's not just you and your child struggling through a situation, although you two may be the only ones present. It's you, your personal history demons, and your child. Unfortunately your child doesn't have a clue he isn't just dealing with "Mommy" or "Daddy." In fact, you may not realize how much of your frustration is due to your own internal battle going on between the present and your memories (conscious and unconscious). This includes how it was done to you, the current situation at hand, how you'd like it to be (your own expectations), how you'd like to handle it today, and what your parents might think about how you want to handle it today. The room is actually emotionally charged and crowded, and the struggle is more complicated than it appears.

Strategies

- **When you're feeling stuck about what to say or do, when you're about to say something you don't want to be saying, quickly give yourself a time-out.** Take a time-out, even if it's only a minute to breath deeply. You may have the luxury of going into another room for a little while if there is another adult around to make sure your child is safe. If you are the only one home and you can't leave your child alone, you may simply want to say, "I need a time-out so I can do this differently. I really want to be loving right now." Sometimes just hearing yourself saying, "I need a time-out" is enough to clue you into slowing down and responding from a different place.

- **When you're stuck, remind yourself of how you want to respond.** Form a complete picture with details of how you want to look as you're responding, what you want to say and how you want to feel. You'll be rehearsing your behavior in your mind and it'll be easier to do in real life.

- **Slow yourself down so you can react differently.**

- **Ask yourself, "How important is this?"** After you decide the relative importance, alternatives will kick in.

- **When in doubt, ask for help.**

- **If necessary, decide to deal with it later.**

Take Care of Your Own Issues

If you were hit, spanked, yelled at, or abused as a child, then during these highly frustrating, tense times when your "darling" small child is testing your limits, and your limits are frayed to begin with—watch out! These are danger zones, where you're most likely to do what you unconsciously and consciously remember. Your memories may be exactly the kinds of scenes you promised yourself you would never inflict on another human being. Take a time-out and get yourself to create the scene the way you want to parent your child today. Separate your present-day self from your yesterday self.

If you get stuck in an old automatic loop, you can get upset by judging your actions and words and being angry at yourself for contemplating or doing what you had promised yourself you never would. So now you're frustrated with your child's behavior in the here and now; upset, angry, or disappointed with your own behavior in the here and now; mourning or angry that your past is infringing on the present; and generally stuck.

If you grew up in an alcoholic home, every community in the country has Al-Anon meetings, and most even have special Al-Anon meetings for people who grew up in alcoholic homes called, "Adult Children of Alcoholics" (ACA or ACOA) meetings. Although Al-Anon was originally formed as a support group to help family members and friends of alcoholics, some meetings are open to people who grew up in dysfunctional homes even where alcoholism wasn't present, because the resulting problems are so similar. People often find, after going to meetings for a while, that there was more drinking involved in their family of origin than they had originally consciously remembered.

Al-Anon meetings can be enormously helpful, cost nothing, and are usually available throughout the day and evening. Check your local phone directory or call information and ask for the Al-Anon number nearest you. When you talk with them, ask them to send you a meeting schedule. Pick a convenient meeting and go. Sometimes people find it really difficult to walk into those rooms for the first time. They're scared of what they'll find.

What you'll find is some people similar to you, who want to untangle themselves from their past, and who want a better quality of life for themselves and their families. Anonymity is an important part of the Al-Anon program, so don't worry about gossip outside of meetings or people "hearing" that you went. "Who you see here, what you hear here, when you leave here, let it stay here," is a saying that is greatly respected and adhered to among Al-Anon members.

If something in your parental bag of tricks needs fixing, use the resources at your disposal such as a therapist, a parent support group, or parenting classes. You're not alone. That's why the outside resources are available. If you need them, take full advantage of them and congratulate yourself for having the courage to go, learn, and grow.

A Bag of Tricks

Short of using outside support resources, there are some things you can do to untangle yourself and diffuse the situation. A phone call to another parent as a way of gaining a different perspective, a break, or advice and support might be the best thing for you. A nice relaxing bath may help. You can even invite your child in so you can both calm down.

Help from a partner may be unavailable, but if your partner is available either in person or by phone, use him or her for some relief or a more objective perspective. Your child may continue to be uncooperative. So what do you do? Some parents suggest praying—that seems to work for them.

All the parents involved in this book thought this was an important chapter, because no matter how well you want to parent, no matter how good your intentions are, no matter how well you really do parent, sooner or later, you will go through those parental testing days. Just as the sounds radio stations make when they test their emergency broadcast systems can jar your body, wait to see how jarring your "wonderful" toddler or 2-year-old can be. I hope that the suggestions contained on these pages will help by providing you with a broader perspective on your situation when you're feeling stuck. All parents have been there.

If you can't reach a friend when your frustration is mounting to a breaking point, try opening to this chapter during times of extreme stress. You may find a solution. Some parents have literally made a grab bag. Take the suggestions offered in this chapter, write each on a piece of paper, put them in a bag, twist the top, and put it in a convenient location (the kitchen or laundry room). When in doubt, pull out a suggestion and try it out. If it doesn't work or doesn't appeal to you, pull out another. Just the act of using the bag may lighten your spirits and enable you to deal with your child differently.

The best advice is to have fun. Lighten up. This is only one moment in both your lives. Whatever you are going head-to-head about probably isn't that important in the greater scheme of things. Step back. Give both of you the room to reconsider your ultimatums and your rigidly held positions. When you do that, watch the tension melt. Time-outs are marvelous inventions. When parents use time-outs to figure out how else they could be handling a situation and emerge with creative, calm ideas, the children seem to need them less frequently.

Grab Bag Suggestions

If you're going to make a grab bag, here's a beginning list of what to put in the bag. Put one suggestion on each piece of paper:

- Keep things simple.
- Prioritize. Think and do first things first.
- Look at the bigger picture.
- Lighten up.
- Back off and let the argument dissipate on its own.
- Back off and let your child cool off on his or her own.
- Detach a little and let your child find his or her own solution.
- Be a comforting or sympathetic parent rather than an all-knowing problem solver.
- Know your own and your child's low energy times and plan your schedule around them.
- Ask yourself, "How can I be flexible now?"

- Apologize as soon as you realize you're behaving or speaking in a way you don't like. It usually stops a downward spiral.
- Have food prepared in advance for stressful or rushed times.
- Take a parental time-out.
- Look at the situation with a sense of humor.
- Take a warm bath.
- Wash your face.
- Take a walk with your child.
- Punch pillows together.
- Bang pillows onto a mattress.
- Call a friend.
- Speak with a partner or spouse.
- Call a crisis line.
- Raise your eyes toward the sky and say, "Help!"
- Tell your child that you don't like how things are going and you'd like to change it.
- Ask your child if she likes how things feel right now and if she says no, then say, "Me neither... Let's figure out a way to feel more peaceful. Can you help?"
- Remember that both you and your child are human.

When the interviews in this book were done, I asked parents to be honest and talk about what they do when their best parenting techniques don't seem to be working. Even though the ideas behind respectful parenting are sound and work a lot of the time, these methods will not result in perfect parent-and-child interactions. All parents and all children are human. Part of being human is being imperfect. Life is challenging sometimes. Parenting is often a challenge. Parents need to take their creativity and their common sense to their fullest potential when they are faced with frustrating situations.

What the Parents Say

As you read the following examples, jot down some other ideas for your grab bag.

Cindy: My frustration comes in when I get into this head space where I'm telling myself, "I should be able to redirect this behavior," only I can't. And the more I'm in there, trying as hard as I can to redirect the situation, the more frustrated I become and the more intransigent my daughter becomes. When I can realize I'm stuck, getting more stuck by the minute, and can back off to give both of us breathing space, the better we do. It's like we're both trapped in a corner (so to speak) with no way out unless one of us, and usually it has to be me, recognizes the situation and goes, "Oh, there's a roomful of space behind me. I don't need to stay trapped in this corner with you. I'll just slowly take a few steps back. There, now I can see a bigger picture. I get it. That wasn't working."

Sometimes retreat and quiet is the most heroic and useful way through a frustrating situation. When I do that, we both calm down, reevaluate our struggle and can offer each other alternatives. Sometimes I need to realize that I can't redirect this behavior. I need to stop trying and just wait this one out. But not when we're in the corner, verbally duking it out. At that point we're both lost in the emotional intensity and neither of us can see a way out.

Bonnie: I get really frustrated when those old voices in my head start saying things like, "I'm obviously not good enough to rectify this situation." When I can hear that old voice and consciously counter it with, "No, that's not true. What *is* true is her frustration. She's entitled to being frustrated sometimes. I'm her mother, and that's all."

I'm not supposed to always make it better or take away her emotional discomfort, otherwise how will she learn to take care of herself when I'm not around? I have to detach sometimes. Not try to fix it. Let it be hers. And know I'm being a good mother. That takes some talking to myself and countering those old negative messages I picked up in my youth.

Sylvia: Sometimes I get frustrated because I don't know if I can laugh at something or if I need to be serious. Like the other day, my son who's almost 3 was playing in the cat's litter box. He was digging with the shovel. I immediately saw  the humor and had to hold back from laughing because I was afraid if I did, he'd do it again and not understand my explanation of why he couldn't do that. I know he loves playing with sand, and the shovel was right there . . .

Instead of laughing, I explained, using a serious tone of voice, that the cat box was off limits, it was actually dirty and needed to be handled carefully by an adult with gloves on, or we could get sick from it. He didn't quite get it. As he questioned me, I became more serious. I think he finally did get it, because he hasn't played in there since.

The majority of my frustration came later as I second-guessed myself, wondering if I could have handled it differently (meaning better) and realizing I'm really unsure about when I can use humor and when I have to be the "Mommy" à la my mother's style. It's frustrating. Talking to friends helps, but I don't always have the time.

Linda: One day when my 2½-year-old daughter and I were really into it, arguing away, each adamantly sure she was right, I just stuck my tongue out at her. It wasn't a deliberate thing or anything. I guess I had seen my kids do it to each other or friends often enough and had done it with my siblings, so that it was there someplace and out it came. My daughter looked shocked for a millisecond, and then we both cracked up laughing. It completely diffused the situation. I kind of like that solution for every once in a while. I may try it again.

Sylvia: Mealtimes at our house can be an excellent opportunity for frustration. Let's say my son is finished eating, or more likely he's pausing and we're still eating. He wants us to pay attention to him, while we'd like to have a few minutes of adult conversation. Obviously a conflict in the making.

One day, my son was sitting on his dad's lap, and started waving his hands in front of his dad's face. His dad warned him to stop or he'd have to get down. Our son didn't listen and kept waving his hands, annoying his dad. Finally his dad said, "You're bugging me, please get down until after I finish eating. Then you can sit in my lap again."

After he finished eating, our son came up to him and asked, "Can I bug you now?" We laughed. It's those wonderful, humorous, spontaneous remarks that can diffuse a tense situation, and come at the most needed times. I love when things like that happen.

Cindy: Sometimes, when I realize something is becoming much more important to me than to my daughter, I try to tell myself, "I'm not going to make a big deal of this." It works with most things. One area in which it consistently doesn't seem to work is her room. I can tell myself for about a week, "It's no big deal, it's her room, if that's how she wants to have it." But ultimately, after about a week, I go in and clean it. Am I giving in or making myself comfortable? I wish I could extend my ability of not making a big deal of things to her room. At least we've eliminated the arguments, but in reality she's just waiting me out, and then I quietly clean it. Not the perfect solution, but it's how things are right now.

Bonnie: When I've had an upsetting or frustrating time with my 13-month-old daughter, I try to take some time and rationally create in my mind the "bigger picture." After all, what is really happening here? Is this particular argument, power struggle, or independent move worth so much within the greater scheme of her life and mine? By looking at the bigger picture—her life, my life—I usually drop what it was I was feeling so adamant about. It's not that important. It also helps me when I can talk about it with my husband later and get his support about my earlier dilemma and my resolution of it.

Cathy: There are times when I've had to discipline or stop my son from doing something when he's been frustrated either by what he was trying to do, or by being stopped before he wants to stop. Afterward, I feel like the mean Mommy. I know that probably stems from wanting so much to do it differently than my mother did it with us when we were younger.

In any event, when those things happened I used to try and make up for it later, feeling like I had to do something really special so he wouldn't see me as a mean Mom. It helped when you presented the perspective of seeing my later actions as balancing the day, rather than having to do something really special to make up for what had happened.

Really, most of the time what happened to make me feel like a mean mom was that I set appropriate limits, which he had been warned about or which had been negotiated with him earlier. So wanting to have a pleasant time later, rather than pushing to do something really special (the old black-and-white thinking a lot of us raised in dysfunctional homes have inbred in us) is a more respectful, healthy approach. I sometimes forget about balance. And when I do, I become frustrated.

Bonnie: Sometimes when I get into a hard place with my young daughter, I have to stand back and reevaluate my goals. I often find my goals are unrealistic. I'm getting frustrated by trying to attain unrealistic goals. One of my unrealistic goals is wanting my daughter to be happy all the time. Another unrealistic goal is trying to be the perfect mother to make up for how I was mothered. And my other unrealistic goal is trying to do too much in too short a time and then getting angry because my daughter is not going along with an unrealistic adult time schedule.

I try to look at the frustrating situation and see what my goal is, decide if it's realistic, and go from there. When it's one of these unrealistic goals, I can kind of laugh at myself, let it go, and go on. My tension and frustration dissipate when I realize I'm being unrealistic and I can simply back off.

Kate: My husband travels a lot with his job, sometimes he's away for three- and four-day stretches. I've found I need to keep things simple when he's gone. Dinners aren't elaborate, but they're nutritious. I try to keep everything we do as simple as possible, asking myself along the way, "Does this really have to happen right now?" or "What happens if I don't do this right now?"

If I don't overburden myself with "things to do" and concentrate on the essentials like enjoying my son, I'm okay. If I start doing too much by the time my husband gets home, I can meet him at the door and say, "Bye, see you," and I'm out of there. And that's not fair to him. He's been working hard those three and four days, too. So, when I remember to keep it simple, our family runs a lot more smoothly when he's gone and when he returns home.

Cathy: I've learned that the afternoons, especially late afternoons, are a low energy time for my son and for me. It's the time we're most likely to get frustrated with each other. Preparing dinner used to be a major source of frustration. He needed my attention. I needed to be cooking. I solved that frustration by preparing our dinner meal before noon. At that time he's full of energy, often entertaining himself or joining me in preparing the meal. Then, in the late afternoon, when we're both tired, drained, and most likely to get into it, I just have to pop something in the stove or microwave and our meal is cooking smoothly and usually served without any frustrating experiences. It's been a wonderful solution.

Bonnie: I'm the kind of person who has always liked finishing something once I've started, like a letter or cooking a meal. It was difficult for me at first because I'd be in the middle of something and my daughter would wake up from a

nap, or want to nurse, or cry. I believed in responding immediately, but there were times I responded with annoyance or
frustration because I was being interrupted. I quickly realized my responses were absurd. I learned it's okay not to
finish things. I've been getting less rigid and more flexible over the last ten years or so, but having this wonderful little baby girl has taught me and pushed me
into being much more flexible than I knew I could
be . . . and so much faster than I would have gotten to on my
own.

Now, if I know I want to eat a meal at a certain time, I'll
start two hours before, even if it's a simple meal because I
want to leave time for interruptions to play, nurse, or soothe
her as she needs or wants. If I finish early, fine, but with the
extra time, I can relax and enjoy her and what I'm trying to
do without feeling frustrated.

Linda: Diaper changing is often a hard time for us. My
daughter doesn't like her diaper being changed. She moves
around a lot and protests while I'm changing her. In the
mornings I'm fine and stay calm easily, knowing this has to
get done and it's too bad she doesn't like it. But a couple
of times now, in the late afternoon I've yelled at her to
stay still. I realize immediately it's ridiculous for me to
lose my temper with her because she's squirming and
making it difficult for me to diaper her. Both times I've
apologized immediately and talked it through with
her, telling her "Mommy's sorry she yelled but
sometimes it's hard for me to stay patient when I
have to change your diaper and you keep moving
around, making it harder to change you and making the whole process longer and worse than it has to be." I
feel better after I've apologized and explained. And she
seems to listen.

It's easier when my husband is home because then one of
us plays and distracts her while the other changes her diaper, and that helps. Then she's not fussy.

Bonnie: Sometimes I feel like my needs conflict with my
daughter's. Like when I'm hungry and she needs to nurse.
Or she needs to nurse and I need to sleep. At times like that,

especially if my blood sugar is low, I can feel the irritation well up inside me. I can stop it if I remember that she has a job to do at this time in her life, and her job is being a baby and voicing her needs. I have a job too, and my job is being her mother and taking care of her needs. We really aren't in conflict, we're complementary.

One solution we've worked out is that my husband makes me a sandwich when he makes his in the morning before leaving for work. That way, if she's hungry and needs to be nursed, and I'm hungry and need to eat, I can eat the sandwich he made while she nurses. I used to put her down and she'd cry for five minutes (which I didn't believe in and which really jarred me) while I made myself a sandwich. Now we both get to eat at once.

I don't really like it when those old feelings from my childhood well up automatically, but at least I can use the new thinking I've picked up along the way to stop the old messages and deal with her the way I want to today. When I don't catch them, I try to deal with the guilt that inevitably seems to arise when I think I haven't been the perfect mother.

Sarah: At times when I find myself going head-to-head with my 2-year-old son over something, anything, what to wear, what to eat, or how to play with him, I'll simply say, "You know what? Mommy needs a time-out. I'm getting frustrated right now because we're disagreeing and neither one of us is giving in. I'm just going to go in the next room for a minute so I can reconsider the situation and calm down. I'll be right back." The reality is, he usually follows me in, so I don't really get a time-out. But it's kind of a time-out, because he's usually quietly hovering rather than pursuing the argument. It serves the purpose of stopping or at least pausing the power struggle.

I've learned I don't have much time before he starts in again, but I can usually quickly take a few deep breaths and get back to feeling my age instead of being right there in the throes of a 2-year-old's power struggle.

It's funny, when I first tried this method and he followed me in, I tried to get him to leave me alone so I could get a "true" time-out all by myself . . . but it backfired and we started arguing about him leaving me alone. It seemed easier for me to give up on the idea of a time-out alone and settle for a time-out where I could bury my head if need be, and he could hover quietly for at least 20 seconds and give me a little bit of breathing space.

If I had stuck with my picture of what a time-out would be for me, I would never have gotten any relief at all. And then I'm not sure where I would be. Would I like more time? Sure, but since he can't seem to give me more, I'll take what I can get and use it as best I can. I think that's part of respecting his limits, too. He can't seem to allow me an alone time-out, but he can give me a little quiet time. I've discovered that's workable. I can do what I need within his limits.

13

Life Wasn't Going To Change This Much...

Can you remember back to a time when having a good night's sleep was the norm rather than a rare event? Remember when it would take a particularly stressful set of events to interrupt your sleep? Or a neighbor was having a loud party, but instead of being upset you wanted to be invited? Or you and your partner were into a particularly passionate period? Remember before having a child when you would sit around and daydream about what your life as a parent with your own family would be like?

Bill Cosby had a wonderful comedy routine years ago about his pre-child imaginings. To paraphrase him: We were going to go skipping through a field of wildflowers in slow motion. My wife, my child, and I. Our faces would radiate love in slightly out-of-focus soft pastels. Like in those artsy films. The sun would be shining. I'd be holding my wife's hand on one side and my child's on the other. Instead, when we had our first baby, reality hit. Family life was far from a romantic, hazy, slow-motion film of a small family in a field of wildflowers. The baby cried, we were exhausted, nobody had the energy for running anywhere, slow motion or not.

What were your dreams, your musings, your ideas, your ideals? How do they compare with life today? Do you even have free time to imagine and compare? After your child goes to bed? Or are you too tired then? Have you gotten any good laughs from what you thought versus what is? Because I'm sure your life is different. Maybe it's not what you thought it would be, but it is different!

People seem to approach parenthood with one of eight primary patterns:

- Panic-stricken: "Oh, no! What are we getting ourselves into?"
- *Laissez-faire* (with varying amounts of confidence): "It'll be okay."
- Rigid: "I know exactly how this will be. I'll still be working, we'll have a nanny so I can continue working, knowing my child is getting quality one-on-one care."
- Sure-footed: "Life won't be changing that much . . . I'm not going to let a little child tell me how to run my life."
- Relaxed, confident, flexible: "I haven't a clue. I'll figure it out as I go."
- Simplistic, positive, loving: "I just want to be a loving and patient parent."
- Idealistic and humane: "I'll never hit my child and rarely if ever yell. It's just not necessary."
- Knows-what-doesn't-want: "I won't be one of those completely devoted parents whose child becomes the center of their universe."

All the parents interviewed for this book said something like, "Most of my original ideas didn't pan out. I had to wing it once my baby was born. I didn't know my ideas would be so far off. I was pretty sure I knew myself well and how I'd react, but once our baby arrived (or soon after our baby arrived) it was clear our prebaby notions of family life just weren't going to apply."

How has it been for you? How do you feel about abandoning or modifying your original plans? Did you have trouble giving them up? Are you surprised with life as it is, rather than how you imagined life would be? What has surprised you?

Be Open

If you're reading this book as you're getting ready to start a family, my recommendation is: Don't have expectations of this child, yourself, or even your mate. Let your family life develop as it will, given the uniqueness of all of you involved. From all the parents I talked to, it's clear that family life has turned out to be different from what they had imagined. They also reported that the stronger their preconceived notions, the more difficult it was for them to give them up and be creative with the situation at hand.

Most families said the mother's life had changed more significantly than the father's life. Somehow the mother was more readily able to give up things like sports or working out. Her schedule, especially when nursing, was affected more than the father's. That is not to say that fathers' lives did not change, just that mothers found their life changed more. When interviewing couples, fathers agreed, especially in cases where the father was the main bread winner. "Acceptance of what is," is a great base for parenting respectfully. And laughing at the differences, the so-called intrusions that don't fit into your preconceived notions, helps enormously.

In this chapter, parents share some of their perceptions of how their lives have changed. The examples are often humorous, sometimes touching, sometimes surprising. All the parents I interviewed found they had cut back on a lot of things they used to do, such as camping, movies, dinners out, romantic evenings, making love, golf, reading, working out, cleaning, or skiing. They truly didn't mind. Instead, they all talked about how much their children had added to their lives. They used terms like, "meaning," "joy," "love," "satisfaction," "appreciation," and "richness." After all, what's a few less tennis games when you're getting (happily) out of shape watching your infant turn over for the first time?

At a recent parent support group, where the topic had been "Adjusting to a New Baby," a few Moms were talking informally afterward, and their conversation went something like this:

"I can't believe it's been almost seven years since I went camping. I mean *camping*—backpacks, tents, that kind of thing. We used to do that all the time."

"I used to love camping. I had even built up the courage to go camping by myself. It was so great! I never went backpacking, just car camping."

"You did? I used to borrow friends' dogs to go camping, but I never went all by myself. Now if my girls were to want to do that, I'm not sure what I'd do. Things were different when I was doing it."

"We used to camp a lot, too! I can't believe that I find myself driving down the highway now, looking enviously at those trucks with camper shells over them, or even some of those big old recreational vehicles I used to put down so much when my husband and I were in our cute little two-person backpacking tent. I never thought I'd see any value to those gas guzzlers. But I'm telling you, I'd love to have one. I could see us camping again if we had one of those."

"We bought one this year."

"You did?"

"Yeah, we actually did. Not one of the big ones. Ours is a pop-up tent trailer. But it has heat, hot water, and its own bathroom. I decided between my getting up at night, and my child's needs, I wanted to camp, but tenting—it didn't sound appealing. I wanted some conveniences like hot water for washing my face. You know, I just wanted it to be a little easier since I knew camping with a child would already make it a little harder."

"Hey, how many does it sleep?"

And they all laughed as they invited themselves to share the camper. After their camping conversation, they talked about some other humorous changes they had experienced since becoming mothers. Then they went on to talk about their children. Their enjoyment was so apparent, it truly shined through.

What the Parents Say

Bonnie: When I was contemplating getting pregnant, I had a difficult time imagining how a child would fit into my busy life. It was more than busy; it was full. I was content with my lifestyle and had been for a long time. I remember saying to my husband, "I can't imagine how life will be if we have a child. But I can't imagine even more being old and not having an adult child around. So I guess if I want the benefits of an adult child, I have to go through the little child part."

He was more ready than I was. He didn't seem bothered by not knowing how we'd fit a baby into our lives. He was confident that when a baby arrived we'd figure it out.

My mother reassured me that not knowing how a baby would fit into my life shouldn't stop me from having a child, because once a baby arrived I'd figure it out. She was confident in my abilities to do so. Someone else suggested that if I didn't try to imagine how a baby would fit in, I'd probably be a better parent because I wouldn't have preconceived notions and I'd be able to "roll with the punches" more easily. That sounded reasonable to me.

I went with the no-expectations formula. I didn't spend time imagining what it would be like. I did, however, have some definite ideas popping into my head of what it *wouldn't* be like: I *knew* I wouldn't be this doting, joyful, appreciative mother, enraptured by her infant, baby, toddler, 2-year-old. Not me. I was a "Career Woman"—I had my own interests! A stay-at-home mom? Never. Not this woman! A wannabe-stay-at-home mom? Not me. But guess what? I became this enraptured, enthusiastic, caring, giving, loving Mom who has refused to acknowledge any "favorite time" of my child's life because it has all been terrific.

When people have said, "Your son is how old?" invariably they reply enthusiastically, "That was my favorite age!" I quietly wonder to myself, "So if that was your favorite age, has it been downhill from there for you?" I don't get it. Any stage of development in front of my face has been interesting, and usually intriguing, exciting, and challenging to boot. See what I mean about reality being different from expectations, even the nonexpectation kind?

Has my life changed? Enormously! In ways I couldn't have foreseen. I'm so grateful for the changes. I appreciate my son's presence, because without it, I would still have my old busy life, which I believed was so full and satisfying. From my perspective today, nothing in life has been as satisfying or joyful as watching my child grow and develop. He has inspired me incredibly!

Linda: I remember when my company was having my going-away-for-maternity-leave party. I was going around telling everyone, "Don't worry, I'll be back." I really didn't imagine that I wouldn't. I liked my job a lot. It wasn't a "career," but it was a nice job. Look at me, two and a half years later, pregnant with my second child. I can't imagine going back to work. When did it happen? I think even before she was born. Right before. But me, not working? I just couldn't have seen it as a possibility before. Yet as soon as she was born I knew. I knew I couldn't and wouldn't go back. We were just too close. She needed me. And I couldn't imagine leaving her. Me?

We don't do things without her. I mean, we really don't. I think my husband and I have been out to dinner maybe twice in the last two and a half years. At first we didn't because it would have been too hard on her. And now she's just so much fun. We'd be missing out on her doing something. This is especially true for my husband. He already feels like he misses out on too much because he has to work. So for us, it's not a sacrifice. It's what we want to do. But a few years ago, would I have seen my life like this? Never. We saw all the new movies. I never imagined life would be like this. But it is. And it's great!

Sarah: I've been amazed at how strongly I react, even in the middle of the night, from this place that says, "I need to take care of this, no matter what!" I mean I can rouse myself from a sound sleep, cope with little sleep, and react to the slightest change in noise indicating something is different and better be checked immediately. I was never like that before I had my son. It's this instinctive, primitive drive that takes over. Before I had my son and I would try to imagine what it would be like, I expected to be more detached, that I'd let my husband take care of it. But there's almost a vigilance about my reactions that has surprised me. Yet it feels so natural.

Bonnie: Since my daughter's birth I keep getting better and better at doing what feels right instead of agonizing, intellectualizing, discussing, and deliberating my actions. There's so much less of that. I never imagined it would be this way.

Linda: Having my daughter has taught me to set priorities. Up until last year (before she was born) I always thought, if I could only figure "it" out, I could do it all. Now I know I can't. I liked life in all its boxes and places before. I felt better when I could get life in those manageable boxes...Is it a relief now? Kind of. But now I have to deal with these constant changes. Yet, prioritizing is easier knowing I can't accomplish all I want to, and there is no "it" to figure out.

Kate: Life has changed a lot. I feel a lot closer to my husband since my son's birth. Now we're not just a couple, we're a family too. That seems to have more ties. I think my husband sees this as an opportunity to be with his son in a way his father never was with him. Our son is only 9 months old, and my husband is already talking about fishing and skiing trips they're going to take. I feel like I'm mending stuff from my mom. I'm not sure how I am or why I'm feeling that, but every time I pick him up when he's crying, every time, it feels good, and something feels better inside me too. We'd often get spanked when we were crying. I can't see the sense in that. So, yes, life is changing, for the better from what I can see so far.

Nothing is as simple as it used to be. Not that that's bad. He's been much more of a reward than anything else, but I was always such a spontaneous person. You can't be as spontaneous. Well, you have to think about things like laundry, because now there's a little baby who needs clean diapers and changes of clothes because he's more vulnerable to changes in weather. If you're going on an outing, you have to have all kinds of layers and extra layers in case he poops through them, which involves some planning in advance. I'm learning, but it's just not completely natural for me. But like I say, it's definitely worth it.

Cathy: I think one of the biggest changes I've experienced since my son was born was in recognizing my values about parenting and how that has affected my friendships. I hadn't expected my friendships to change so much. For instance, at work, during breaks when we talked, I was so intrigued with what my child was doing, I often steered the conversation to talking about our kids. And to my surprise and sometimes horror, I found how differently I was parenting than my coworkers who I had considered friends before. When I heard their stories of how they handled their children, I just couldn't be friends with them anymore. I clammed up in horror a few times. It was so uncomfortable. As a result, I've become pretty alienated at work. That's been disappointing.

I just can't be friends with people who parent in certain ways, because I no longer respect them. In fact I'm appalled with how they sometimes treat their children. For instance, one woman I had known a long time, and considered a work friend was talking about her 18-month-old, and said, "Damned if he didn't crawl around, pull the plug in our water bed, and all this water came gushing out. I just went over there, replugged the bed, picked him up, and gave him a spanking. He had been told about that plug. He knew better than that...." Stories like that made me cringe. I just couldn't say anything. Spank an 18-month-old? Spank at all?

I became hungry for people who treated their children with respect and dignity and found myself constantly disappointed. I hadn't realized how important it was to be around people who parent the way I do. And I hadn't realized how widespread yelling and spanking still is today. I realized quickly how strong my values toward respecting children (including infants) were. And although it's been lonely, I've needed and wanted to stick with my newly identified values. It's meant a lot to me, and I think to my son.

Carl: Before I had my son, I had one personal thing in my office, a clay mug I drank my coffee from. That was it. Anything else had been provided by my employer. By the time my son was 4 months old, I had a 2' x 3' photo collage of my son, my wife, and me. And it's been growing since then.

One of the things I started noticing when my son was about 3 months old was that I had become much more tolerant of my coworkers' moods. I had learned about moods from my son. I have always been a rather private person, probably viewed as aloof, standoffish. Most of that was because I had little tolerance for people and their idiosyncrasies, including mood changes. I didn't know how to deal with them. But I found my son's moods so intriguing, so simple, so impersonal, (he wasn't out to get me). He was just being human when he cried or smiled or laughed or stared... It seems to have generalized to my understanding of people. It sure makes my life easier.

≈

Before he was born, I had been afraid about how I'd be, because I knew you were supposed to be able to "be there" for a baby, and I always needed a lot of "alone space." I think my wife and I both figured she'd have to compensate, when I had to "go away." But so far, I haven't had to go away. I've been so intrigued, so involved ... and it feels so good. Maybe those years of therapy have finally come together, and they're clicking in me. He sure is helping though ... in ways I never imagined. I know it's easier to be around me because I'm more tolerant and understanding of other people. And I've learned it from him. He's only 9 months old now. I wonder what else I'll be learning from him.

Steve: Before I became a father I had absolutely no experience with children. We're talking no cousins, no nieces, no nephews. Everything was brand new for me. And let me tell you, the change was all for the better for me. It was difficult for my friends, but easy for me. Let me give you an example. My son was born December 29. For the first few days I just went around saying, "Wow." On New Year's Eve some friends had rented a room in a hotel to have a small private party, maybe 12 to 20 people. The hotel was catering it, and I knew it was going to be a fun nice party. But as the night went on, there I was in the hospital, holding my new baby, or watching my wife nurse our new baby. I started thinking, "I've got a brand new family. It's a new year, and I have a new family. I think I'll stay right here." And I did until around 1:00 a.m.

Then I went home for a few hours of sleep before I went back to greet my new family on New Year's Day. I knew I could have still gone to the party, my friends would have been glad to see me . . . but I just wanted to be with my family, then get some sleep so I could be with my family again. And that was only two days after my son was born. I know that was different behavior for me. My friends didn't understand. But I felt so good about it.

Cindy: My 10-month-old daughter is the most important person in my life. Trying to raise her to be a healthy, confident person as she grows up is what I want to be doing right now. I'm realizing it's the most important thing I can do in my life. My career is on hold indefinitely, and that's fine. We're going to make do with less so I can be home with her. I didn't know I'd feel so strongly about this before she was born, but my decision feels firm and right.

As an infant she wanted to be held and nursed all the time. And I did. After a few months as she began to enter babyhood I had certain expectations that this would change, only it didn't. I read some of Dr. Sears' books and found she fit many of the characteristics of a high-need baby. I found I had to be more patient and put my expectations aside for her. My needs from the past aren't as important as they once were. I can set them aside for her. I didn't know it would be so easy to do.

When my daughter was about 1 year old, my husband and I went on our first date since her birth. We went to the movies. The two of us sat there, watching, and saying quietly to each other, "Wow! This is incredible." We had forgotten what movies looked and sounded like on the big screen. We had been renting videos at home from time to time, but this was something else! It was so big. It was so bright. The sound was so clear. We were actually at the movies. We were actually away from the house, away from our daughter. It had taken one year. Incredible!

I'm glad I was in my middle 30s when I had her. I know I couldn't have given this much 10 years ago. But now, I know I'll have time later. She'll only be this young and this needy for a short time and I can do things like ski later.

Rhonda: I used to need a lot of time to myself. Before my daughter was born, I'd get home an hour before my husband. I'd look forward to that hour alone where I could just  be myself. I didn't have to answer to anyone. I wasn't a professional or a wife...just me. Now...time alone? I never get it. Time for myself? I'm trying to get to an exercise class three times a week where there's child care on the premises...but my daughter isn't doing too well with that. We're trying.

It's amazing that I don't get more frustrated. Maybe because she meets my needs in ways I never thought. There's so many unexpected pleasures I get out of spending every day with her, watching her learn, being there with her. I probably would have been more selfish 10 years ago, but now...this is the best thing that ever happened to me.

Sarah: My husband came home one day, took one look at me and started laughing. I had no idea what was so funny until I looked down at my sweater. There, across and down the length of my navy blue sweater were the white remains of at least four burpings from my month-old child. I do remember thinking, as he spit up for the first time, "I should change my sweater..." But burp number two quickly followed and by number three I figured, "Why bother?" I mean, why dirty two? I was about to explain all this when my still laughing husband said, "You would never have looked like this a month ago..." Ah yes, how quickly life can change.

〰

How did it happen that I may as well not even go into a video rental store because I don't recognize any titles? And when you read the backs of the boxes they all sound great, but you know they're not. You don't want to be bored if you're going to fight your exhaustion and actually stay awake for two hours after your child falls asleep. So rather than be disappointed, you may as well walk out empty-handed.

I mean, I can remember thinking how I certainly would never let my life get so small that I wouldn't know the current movies to see, or six-month-old good movies to rent. Certainly a babysitter at least once a month was in order. Oh, I saw what parenthood did to some people and I wasn't going to fall for it. I was going to be different. My life wouldn't change *that* much.

So how did it happen? It took me till he was 18 months old to even have enough of an outside interest that I thought seeing a film at home might be kind of nice. But by the time I got to the video store a few months later, they were all unrecognizable. And I went home empty-handed.

Okay, so going to the video store didn't work so well. I was going to follow my own advice and get out with my husband at least once a month. No big deal right? Right, except for teething discomfort (how could we leave him?), unreliable babysitters, busy babysitters, and finally success. I had combed the newspapers for reviews. Picked a movie. Looked forward to it. Checked the paper. Arrived at the theater only to find a different movie on the marquee. The paper was wrong! Another time, the movie theater was closed for renovations. Another time the line was long, and by the time we got to the window to buy our tickets, the movie we wanted to see was sold out.

≈

I thought life was full and complete before. I really did. But now, looking back, I can't believe I ever thought that. What my son has offered me has been so much more rewarding than writing a paper, having a project funded, finishing a project, a great ski run, a fun round of golf . . . you name it. My perspective on life has changed so completely.

I don't even mind being out of shape. Someday, when he's older and in school I'll probably get to that. It's just one of those things (like, a clean organized house), I've given up so I can be with him more and enjoy his childhood. It's been incredibly worth it. I wouldn't trade my life today for my life before for anything!

Endnotes

Chapter 2

1. William Sears, *Creative Parenting: How to Raise Your Children Successfully from Birth to Adolescence* (New York: Dodd, Mead and Company, 1987), 94.

2. Ibid., 92.

3. Ibid., 95.

4. Penelope Leach, *Your Baby and Child* (New York: Alfred A. Knopf, 1989), 46.

5. Williams Sears, and Paul Froelich, *Becoming a Father* (Franklin Park, IL: La Leche League International, 1991), 52.

Chapter 3

1. Marianne Neifert, *Dr. Mom* (New York: NAL, 1987), 135.

Chapter 10

1. Joan Kelly, Keynote speech, Colorado State IDC Conference, Vail, CO (2000, May).

Other Resources

Civardi, Anne. *Moving House.* Tulsa: EDC Publishing, 1985.

Freed, Jeffrey, and Laurie Parsons. *Right Brained Children in a Left Brained World: Unlocking the Potential of Your ADD Child.* New York: Simon and Schuster, 1997.

Ricci, Isolina. *Mom's House Dad's House.* New York: Simon and Schuster, 1997.

Santa Cruz Toddler Care Center, Irene van der Zande, Santa Cruz Toddler Care Center Staff. *1, 2, 3 . . . The Toddler Years.* Santa Cruz, CA: Toddler Center Press, 1989.

Wallerstein, Judith S., Julie M. Lewis, and Sandra Blakeslee. *The Unexpected Legacy of Divorce: A 25 Year Landmark Study.* New York: Hyperion Publishing, 2000.

About the Author

Joanne Baum, PhD, LCSW, BCD, CAC III, received her Ph.D. in Social Welfare from the University of Wisconsin in 1979. She has been working in family therapy since 1974. Dr. Baum is a licensed clinical social worker, board certified in clinical social work, and a level-III certified alcoholism counselor. Joanne writes parenting columns for *The Canyon Courier* in Evergreen, Colorado, and has written two books on substance abuse. She has a private practice outside of Denver, Colorado, where she lives with her family. Dr. Baum, M.O.M., has been a mom since 1990—and that is her favorite title.